Johnny White's SPORTS BAR

The Tiny Joint that Never Closed—Until It Did

MARITA WOYWOD CRANDLE

Foreword by J.D. Landrum

THE History PRESS

Published by The History Press
Charleston, SC
www.historypress.com

Front cover, top left and bottom left images courtesy of the author. Front cover, top right and bottom right images courtesy of Moriah Blue. Back cover images courtesy of the author.

First published 2018

Manufactured in the United States

ISBN 9781467140904

Library of Congress Control Number: 2018952847

Notice: The information in this book is true and complete to the best of our knowledge. It is offered without guarantee on the part of the author or The History Press. The author and The History Press disclaim all liability in connection with the use of this book.

In wine there is wisdom
In beer there is freedom
In water there is bacteria

While this quote was once thought to have been written by Benjamin Franklin, the true author remains unknown.

This book is dedicated to all those who loved and lived
Johnny White's Sports Bar

Contents

Contents

Foreword

I remember meeting Marita briefly in the fall of 2002. A nice-looking German gal from California. She was with Lucinda, one of our part-time bartenders. I say briefly, because the look on her face said it all, like she just stepped in dog poop. We got that look a lot. Months later, she was tending bar and, not long after that, managing. Guess that poop didn't smell so bad after all.

The three original owners were Terry Frantz, Tom Hill and me. The "Three Amigos," or maybe more like "The Three Stooges." We each had other jobs. Terry worked for Amtrak out of Chicago, and Tom was a well-known contractor, having done quality jobs in the Bywater and the French Quarter. He built Johnny White's Sports Bar in four days.

Myself, just a country boy from Conroe. I worked part-time as a realtor and tended bar at the original J.W.'s on St. Peter Street. I'm not sure what motivated Tom or Terry to open a bar, but my motivation was eight pounds, six ounces—my son, Lance. None of us had much dough. I used credit cards to buy supplies and five, thirty-two-inch TVs, one for each corner of the bar. The plan was to market the bar as a locals' sports bar. I remember thinking we may have more TVs per square foot than any bar in the world, 425 square feet to be exact.

I always thought Terry should have been born in the twenties. A real fast talker who easily made friends and loved New Orleans—sometimes too much, if you know what I mean. He actually had more to do with the bar getting open than Tom or myself. Tom Hill was, well, it's kind of hard to explain. Tom, a hillbilly from West Virginia, knew everybody, and everybody knew him. You always knew when Tom was in the house! We quickly became good friends.

Johnny White's Sports Bar almost didn't happen. I drew up the lease, and we went to submit our paperwork to city hall. We got rejected! The city had passed regulations stating any new bar must have a kitchen. Well, what the hell! The bar was only as big as an average-size bedroom. We decided to change the name to Johnny White's Sports Bar and Grill and resubmit our paperwork. We passed! They never came out to inspect our kitchen. We did have food, sort of—a Crock-Pot full of hot dogs. To this day, I don't think the city cared. They were just happy for the revenue.

In January 1990, there wasn't much going on at Bourbon and Orleans. There were no streetlights, and it was very dark. Most tourists, drunks, turned down St. Peter Street, where Pat O'Brian's, Preservation Hall and the original Johnny White's were located. The bar finally took off a couple of years later because we were the only twenty-four-hour bar on Bourbon, and the bar became a locals' hangout.

I'm not sure why Terry became unhappy after a couple of years, but he found an uptown buyer. It was a very good offer, but Tom and I decided not to sell. It forced us to buy Terry out. Terry found a house in Mississippi and, along with his wife, Shannon, moved. At the time, I thought it was a good move, because like I said, he really enjoyed New Orleans. Sadly, he passed away three years later. He just couldn't give up the drinking. Tom and his wife, Betty, took care of the books, and I ran the daily operations. Tom also enjoyed New Orleans. He was starting to spend more time at the sports bar than home. The good part was that he only lived four blocks away. Betty was concerned with his health and convinced him to move back to West Virginia in 2001.

My friend Lori, who I'd known for thirty-five years, also knew Tom and bought Tom and Betty's shares. Not sure of the amount but certainly more money than I had. Lori was a banker, and I was happy having her as a partner. Thanks, Lori. We later invested in two more properties that did very well. But it all happened because of that tiny little bar on Bourbon. She made it all possible.

I always thought of the sports bar as my girlfriend. A love-hate relationship that is all too common in the French Quarter. She never met a stranger and she had a way of bringing people together. I remember that opening night back in late December 1989. My only customers were Tom, Terry, Richard the artist and myself. We all got drunk of course, celebrating finally getting the bar open. When it became obvious that we were going to be our only customers, we decided to close for the night. There was one big problem—we forgot to make keys to lock up. I had to stay open till 9:00 a.m. waiting for the morning bartender. We never did get around to making those keys.

She became famous after the storm, keeping her doors open for those in need. That's when I was most proud. She passed away at midnight on June 30, 2012. Crowds of old friends and new, along with bystanders wondering what was happening, filled the bar and the streets. We had a traditional second line parade down Bourbon Street, giving tribute and celebrating the passing of our loved one.

It was a sad time, and the whiskey didn't help that night. I remember thinking Tom and Terry should be here.

She had no idea what was happening until the next morning, when the wrecking crew showed up. I did go back to Bourbon and Orleans a few months later. The bar had certainly changed. Some would say for the better. For myself, I just miss her and how she changed so many lives.

She's still there of course, behind all the new paint and sheetrock, if only in my mind. "How you doing kid?"

"I'm OK, J.D. I miss you too. Thanks for the memories."

Walls talk, you know!

—J.D. Landrum

Preface

Drinking Mistakes

When I first moved to the French Quarter, it was meant to be part-time. I rented a small apartment on Royal Street, across from Pirates Alley, because I thought having a place in New Orleans would make me miss the city less while I was away engaged in my "real" life in California. I had a house, two dogs, two cars, and I ran the marketing department for a multimillion-dollar corporation. New Orleans was my escape, but I never found out if using the apartment part-time would make me feel better—because I never left. After about four months of making excuses for not going back to California, I sold my house over the phone, left my job, grabbed my dogs and cars and made New Orleans home.

On one of my first nights in the Quarter, I was looking for a bar to watch the L.A. Lakers play. I ran into my realtor, Terry Foley, who told me about Johnny White's Sports Bar, a locals' bar on the corner of Bourbon and Orleans. I decided to walk by. It was a hole in the wall, at least what I could see of it through the scratched-up, filthy French door windows. It looked dirty, seedy and tiny and was filled with people listening and even dancing to the jukebox. I wanted to watch the game. "I'd never go in there," I thought to myself. That was my first introduction to Johnny White's Sports Bar, the magical little bar that had more personality than it had square feet.

A few nights later, I met my neighbor Lucinda, who told me she had moved out of my apartment and across the courtyard because the ghost there was getting on her nerves. But that's another story. Lucinda invited me to visit her during her shift at Johnny White's for mimosas in the morning.

She worked from 7:00 a.m. to 11:00 a.m. and explained that the bar never closed. Even though I was not impressed with the bar, Lucinda was fun, so I decided to leave the option open.

Morning rolled around, and I was awakened at 7:05 a.m. by Lucinda's screen door slamming shut as she ran down the stairs to make her shift, a sound that became familiar over the next several months.

I decided to give it a go. It was November, so there was a slight chill in the air, my favorite time in New Orleans. I headed down to the bar with some paperwork. Thinking to myself what a strange shift Lucinda had at a bar from 7:00 a.m. to 11:00 a.m., I wondered who could possibly be in there at that time of day. To my surprise, there were several customers. In fact, of the approximately twelve bar stools, only two were vacant. Lucinda made me a mimosa and gave me five dollars to play the jukebox. It was at that moment that this tiny bar that never closed sucked me in.

I found myself visiting Lucinda more and more and celebrating my mornings in New Orleans at Johnny White's. When I met the owner, J.D., an "irresponsible, responsible sort," we decided it would be good to open a blues club together. While the club between us never materialized, it prompted me to request a shift or two at the sports bar because I didn't think it was a good idea to manage bartenders if I'd never tended bar. J.D. thought

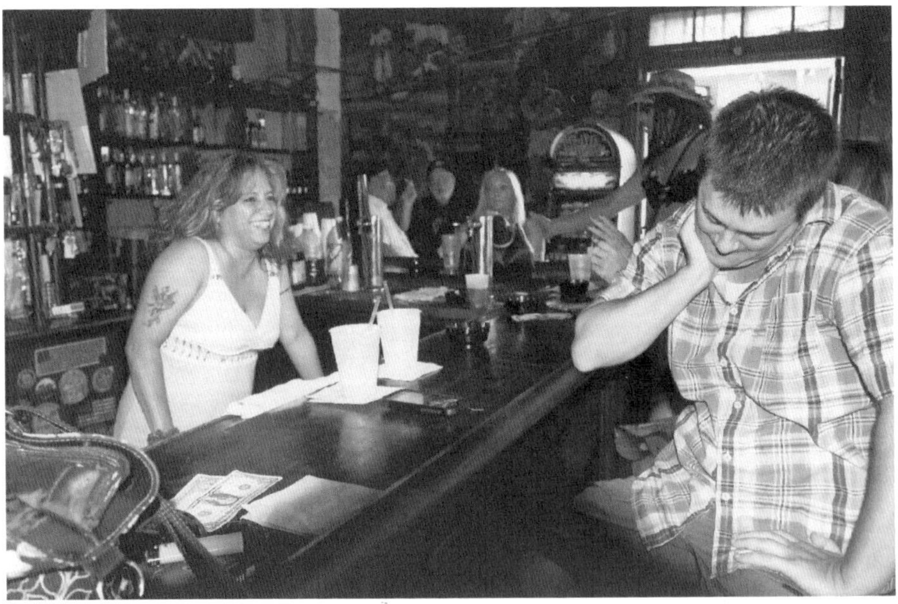

Interior, Johnny White's Sports Bar. *Moriah Blue.*

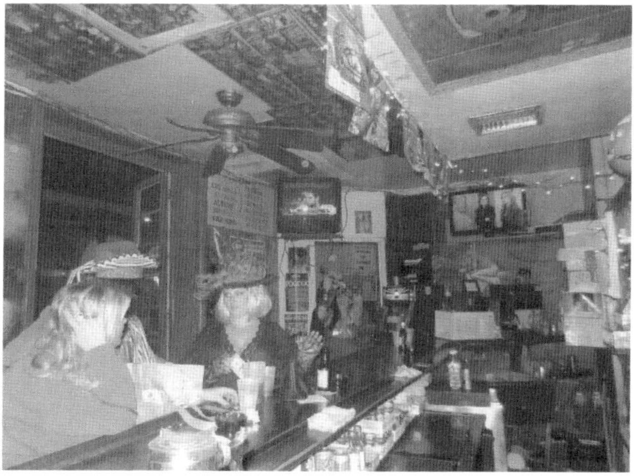

Interior, Johnny White's Sports Bar. *Byron Penn.*

about it for a few days, and I'll never forget the night I got the phone call. "Little girl," he said, "I'm about to put you to work. You ready?" He gave me the graveyard shift from 1:00 a.m. to 7:00 a.m. Thursday through Saturday and Monday nights. I was excited, anxious and nervous all at the same time. I remember having butterflies in my stomach my entire first week. I had spoken in front of hundreds of people in my previous jobs, explaining complicated presentations and here I was nervous about entertaining and making drinks for a dozen or so people. Half of the patrons were welcoming, while the other half resented me for replacing an icon, Tommy Pye, who had manned the graveyard shift there for several years. I couldn't fill his shoes, so I had to create my own. In not too much time, I became one of the gang.

Our little bar was already somewhat infamous, but it was made world famous by Katrina, the real hurricane. Because we never closed our doors, the bar had always been a haven for those who stayed during the storms. Even before my time, the locals created a tradition, throwing tremendous hurricane parties at Johnny White's for those who remained in town during hurricanes and tropical storms. The hurricane parties we had over the years that I was at the bar are some of my fondest memories. In fact, even the news media found refuge at Johnny White's during the aftermath of Katrina. This magical little bar was too big for its britches. Yet there was nothing commercial about it. The mere fact that a bar on Bourbon Street drew this local crowd at all hours of the day was a phenomenon in and of itself. Almost everyone who lives in New Orleans avoids Bourbon Street whenever possible, unless it was to have a drink in "the locals' living room"—Johnny White's.

During my eleven years as a bartender at Johnny White's, I made countless mistake cocktails, which I often enjoyed in the company of my customers. Too precious to simply throw away, there's something very enticing about drinking mistakes. There is, of course, the element of waste not, want not that's instilled in almost every one of us at a very young age, and let's be real—it's free. There are all kinds of mistakes to be made. Sometimes it's because you've made one too many. Then there are the closely named liquor types. "No, I ordered a J&B, not Jim Beam." Or, "I wanted Stoli orange flavor and soda, not Stoli, orange juice and soda." And sometimes people just mumble.

At local bars like Johnny White's, it was easy to make "regular" mistakes. Bartenders count on their regulars being creatures of habit and often start making drinks when they catch a glimpse of one of their regular customers approaching the bar. However, occasionally a regular would get a wild hair and decide to drink a Cuba Libre because they just got done watching *Casablanca.* Or they would order a Sazerac because they had just left one of our street festivals that got them in the mood for local flavor.

There aren't many mistakes I wouldn't drink. I'd try them all, but now and then I'd come across a recipe for disaster, like a tequila mistake on a day I started with whiskey. I'd either give it to someone else or commit the worst case of alcohol abuse and pour it down the drain.

I also enjoyed creating special drinks for various occasions, which just damn near opened the door for making a few mistakes along the way. I usually enlisted the services of one of our regulars as a partner, or guinea pig rather, for tasting. My favorite creations were "The Dewy Decimal" for

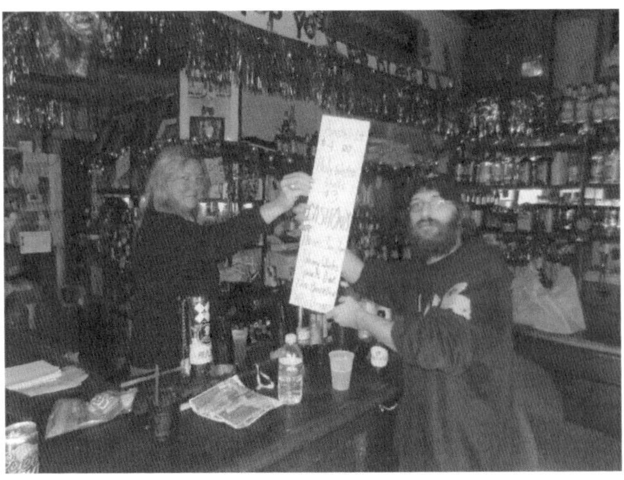

Handwritten cocktail specialty sign about to be placed in the bar's shadow box outside the bar. *Byron Penn.*

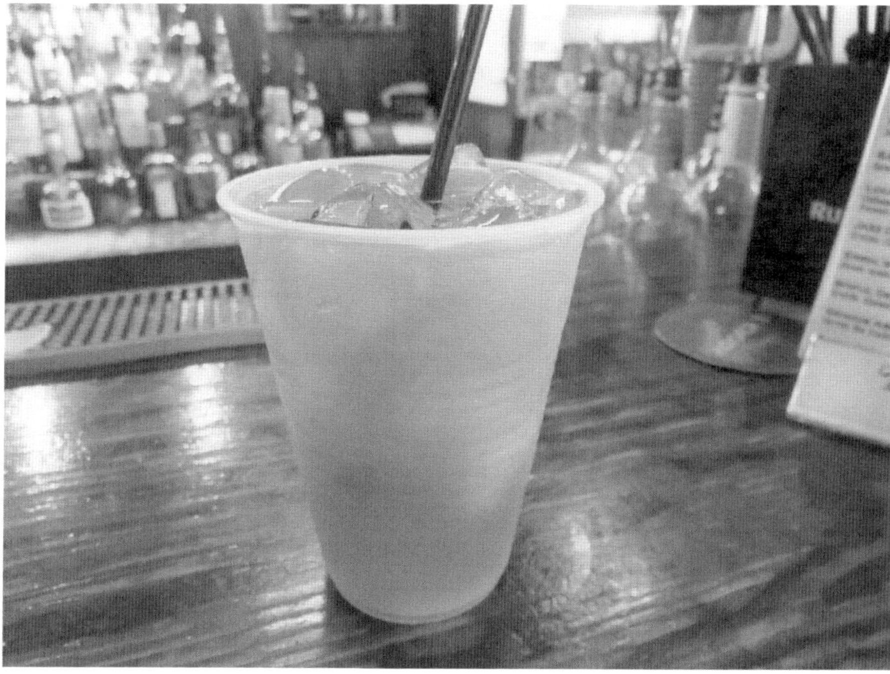

Specialty cocktail Mule Water. *Author's collection.*

the librarians' convention, the "Placebo" for the psychiatrists' convention and "Mule Water" in honor of Dixie the mule and her buggy driver Diane, who always stopped in front of Johnny White's to offer their buggy-load of customers a cocktail from the bar. It seemed only fitting they should have a specialty drink for their customers to enjoy. "Mule Water" only took two mistakes to create.

Mistakes were plentiful, and while sometimes the mistakes were welcome and other times I had dreaded them, I found that with most mistakes came an interesting story, revelation or insight into French Quarter culture.

Acknowledgements

Thank you to J.D. Landrum for giving me the opportunity to be part of the Johnny White's Sports Bar family and for keeping me laughing. Thank you to all the bartenders with whom I worked who helped make our bar a magical place. Thank you to all our customers: locals, regulars and regular tourists whom I know loved the bar just as much as those who worked there. Thank you Elaine Handloff for being my sounding board since this book's inception. Thank you to Jeaneen and Shannon White, Johnny White's daughters, for keeping the legacy going. Thank you Robert Ticknor of the Historic New Orleans Collection for his help with research. Thank you Dawn Kesslering for the unlimited use of her camera. A big thank-you to my editor Amanda Irle for helping to make this book possible.

Introduction

Johnny White's Sports Bar was the tiny Bourbon Street bar that from Labor Day September 1989 to June 30, 2012, was located on the corner of Bourbon Street and Rue Orleans, in the heart of the French Quarter. The bar's original, colorful owners were three guys who took a chance trying their hand at making money with their favorite pastime. J.D. Landrum, Tom Hill and Terry Frantz rented the spot on Bourbon Street from their buddy Johnny White, a popular French Quarter teacher and football coach who already owned a successful bar in the Quarter. Borrowing Johnny White's name, the bar quickly became known as the "locals' living room." Locals were drawn to the spot. Then came the highly sought-after Mardi Gras tapes. These homemade videos of locals and tourists flashing their bosoms, dancing on the bar and enjoying Mardi Gras in New Orleans were played on the television screens in the bar twenty-four hours a day and were also sold to those who wanted to take the fun home with them. Unique to this bar alone, it was *Girls Gone Wild* before its time. Already a destination for locals and tourists from all walks of life, the bar then became world famous when Hurricane Katrina hit New Orleans. The hurricane had even CNN reporters and staff finding refuge at Johnny White's during that very trying time.

Johnny White's Sports Bar (J.W.'s) was the place you would go if you had just had something wonderful happen to you and you wanted to share the news. It was the place you would go if something devastating just happened to you and you needed a shoulder to lean on. There was always

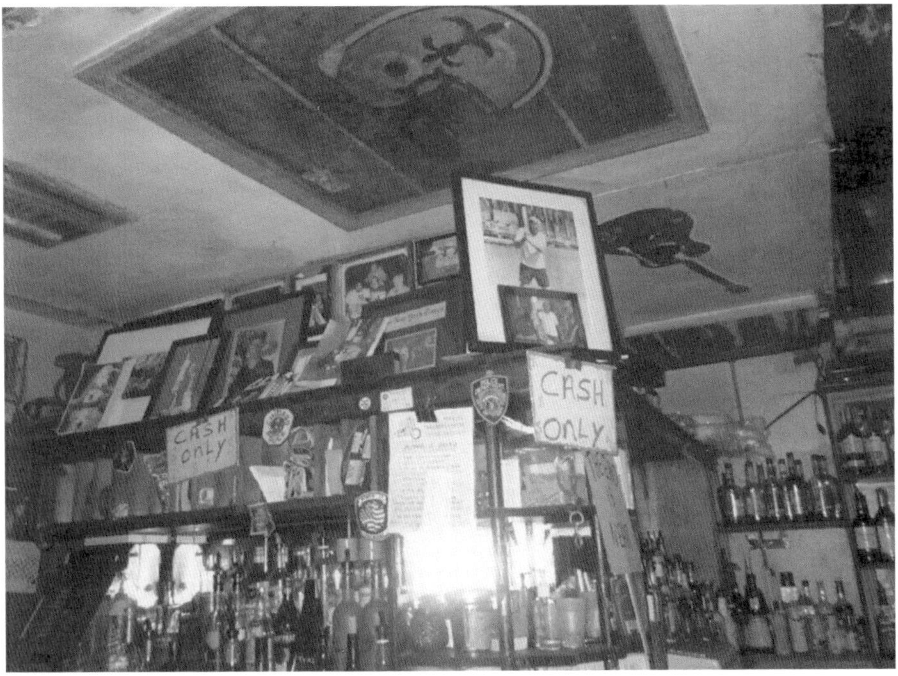

Behind the bar. *Byron Penn.*

someone at J.W.'s you knew and someone who would genuinely care about your news—good or bad.

This bar was the place you could pretty much count on being the scene for some interesting conversation, some thrilling event or even just a game of Scrabble, backgammon or cribbage. Many bartenders would play Scrabble with their customers during their shifts at the bar. Daily, no matter who the bartender happened to be, at 4:30 p.m., it was time for *Jeopardy!*. Everyone would put a dollar in the kitty, and when "Final Jeopardy" commenced, if there was a winner, they would gain the pot. If not, the money would be held until the following evening.

Many locals took their morning coffee at J.W.'s, sometimes with liquor, sometimes without. It was the French Quarter lobby, where locals and tourists often read their morning papers and caught up on any events that took place at the bar the previous night. The graveyard shift welcomed colorful characters and unruly behavior now and then. Hearing it secondhand the following morning was almost as entertaining as having witnessed it the night before.

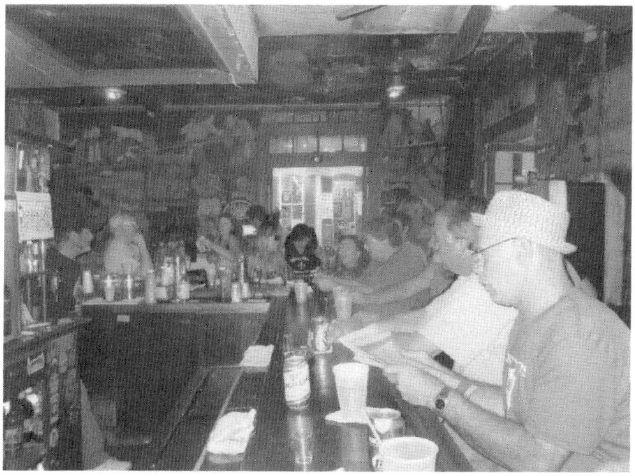

Left: Interior, Johnny White's Sports Bar. *Byron Penn.*

Below: Interior, Johnny White's Sports Bar. *Moriah Blue.*

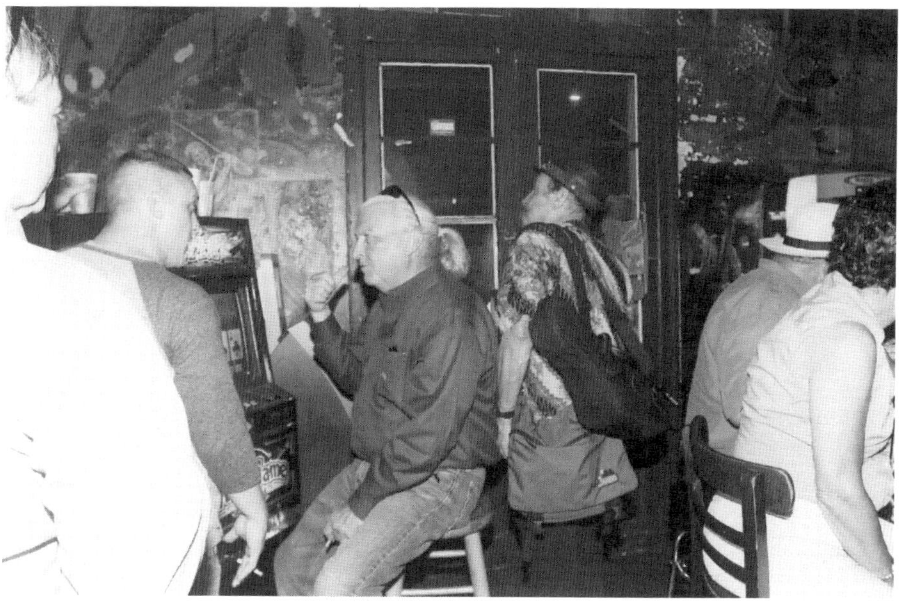

Many tourists, once the bar had stolen their hearts, would arrive at Johnny White's straight from the airport and only after their first few cocktails would they check into their hotels. The bar became their home base during their vacations, and these regular tourists found themselves attracting and cultivating more of the same and planning future rendezvous at J.W.'s with their new friends.

The bar had a real magical quality. While there were thousands of customers who frequented the bar over the years and hundreds of locals who

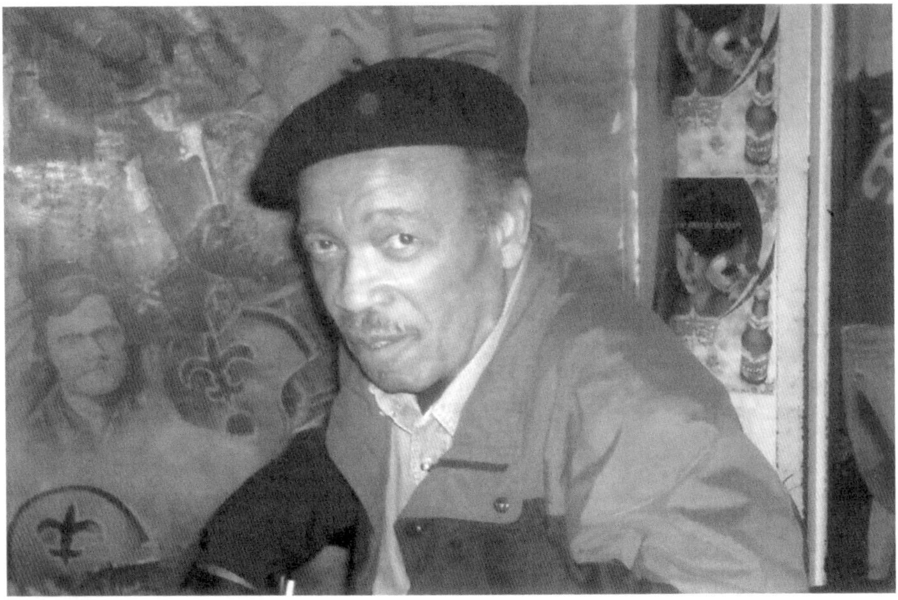

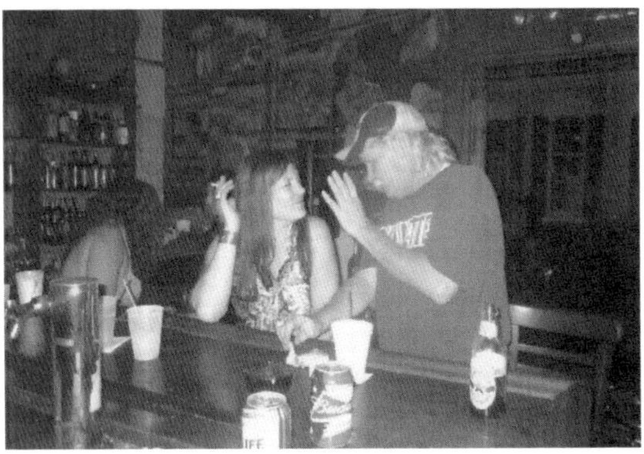

Above: Regular Charlie Sims, owner of Donna's Jazz Club. *Byron Penn.*

Left: Regulars Moriah and Bob "Woof" enjoying a cocktail. *Byron Penn.*

visited often—many visited daily—there were only about twelve barstools. Yet at any visit to J.W.'s, it was somehow possible that a stool was waiting for you or soon available. I found it fascinating and soon stopped questioning it, accepting it as J.W.'s magic. Also, some bartenders and some customers insisted the bar was haunted, and stories of their haunting experiences became the topic of late-night conversation.

The French Quarter has a way of making you feel like you have stepped back into the past and are temporarily leaving reality. Maybe that's why so many tourists go way too far indulging in every vice this city has embraced over centuries. When I embraced Johnny White's Sports Bar, I gained not only a French Quarter family but also a venue for welcoming visitors to

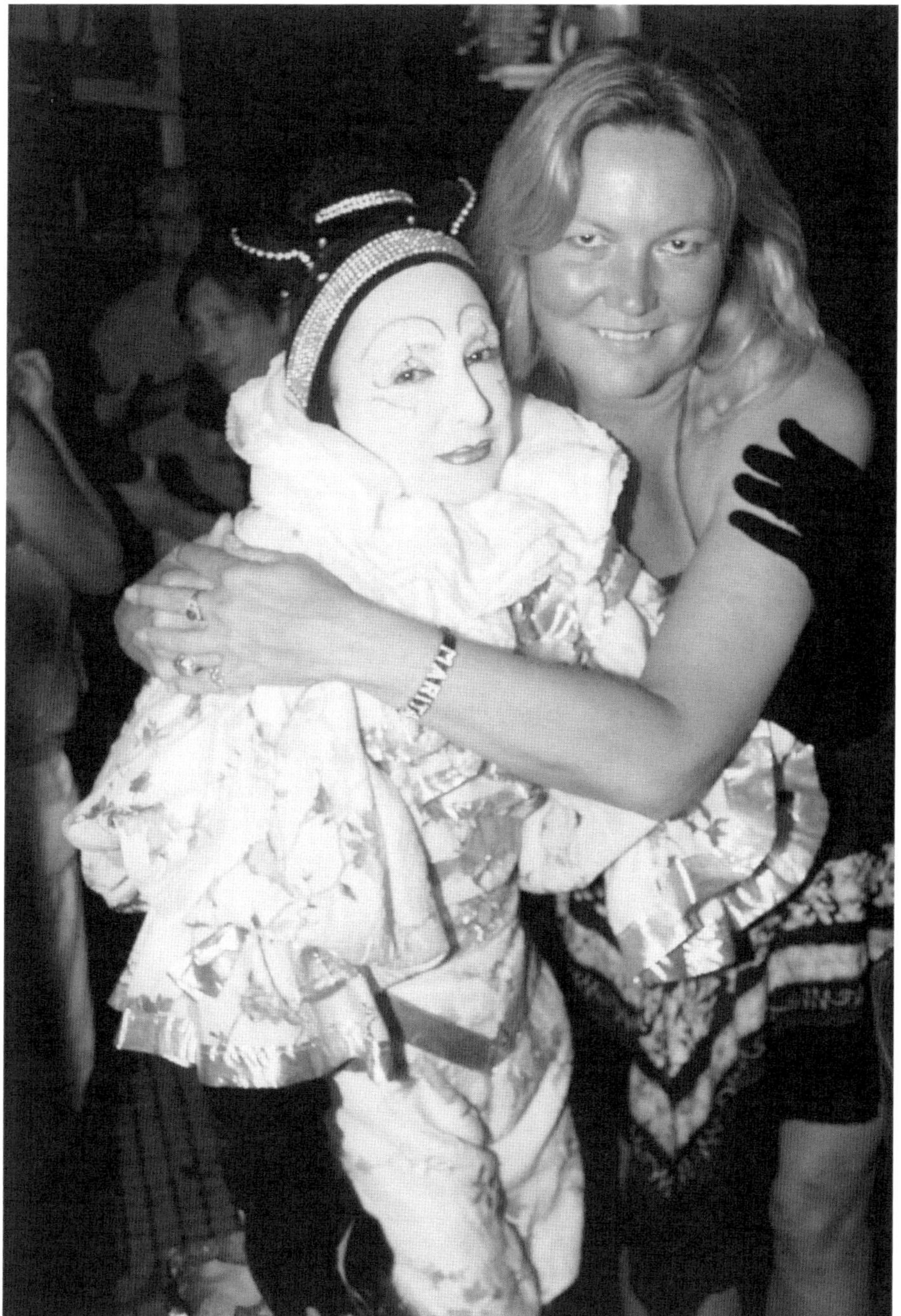

Street performer Suzanne, pictured with J.W. bartender and author Marita Woywod Crandle. *Moriah Blue.*

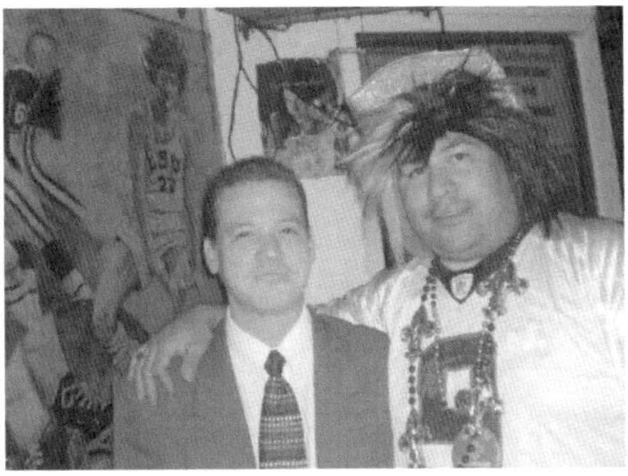

Regulars Freddie (*left*) and Zach in front of a mural of Pistol Pete Maravich. *Byron Penn.*

New Orleans and sharing the city's culture and character. Through the colorful personalities this bar attracted, the bar had a way of winning the hearts of both the staff and our guests, making tourists from all walks of life regulars.

When the lease had ended and unfortunately was not renewed, those who loved the bar lost a friend. While many of its regulars still gather there or at other local French Quarter bars, there is a hole in our hearts for Johnny White's Sports Bar. I, like so many others, found myself mourning the bar. Even after almost seven years now, often we find ourselves longing to return to the rustic walls of J.W.'s. I haven't met a bar yet that has the character or comfort of our locals' living room. I don't know if it's possible to illustrate the bar's importance to the hearts of so many through just a few colorful stories and remembrances, but my words are sincere and heartfelt. I hope this book is a little walk back in time to those who graced the wall of Johnny White's and called it their home away from home. The characters that frequented Johnny White's largely enhanced the charm of the bar. J.W.'s was a place where memorable experiences and stories came easy, and its visitors collected stories to share. The following are a few stories, revelations and hilarities of my recollections of Johnny White's Sports Bar and the people who contributed to what made the bar so unique.

1
The Evolution of Johnny White's

Meet me at Johnny White's! was a phrase heard many times by many people over the years, both locals and tourists alike. A confused look crept across many a customer's faces when they peeped into our little bar expecting to find their friends for a rendezvous and saw only strangers. With four Johnny White locations, newbies to the Quarter could be easily confused, leading to many missed rendezvous, as locals usually simply referred to their favorite as "the" Johnny White's. Often you could tell exactly what a customer was looking for—other times, they would come in with purpose and wait patiently until they were on their second drink, finally complaining about the long wait for their friends. "There are four Johnny White's" we would explain, causing the customer to scurry off to the appropriate location, where their friends waited for them, equally annoyed.

Johnny White was a New Orleans native and a well-liked teacher and football coach at Francis T. Nicholls High School, on St. Claude. In his younger years, he lived above his original Johnny White's, located at 733 St. Peter Street. It was a real local dive bar with a few poker machines in the back; pictures of locals filled the walls, and some locals became part of the furniture. He is said to have been the kind of person people liked to be around by all who knew him, including former bartender Byron Penn. "The bar could be completely empty on any given day," said Penn. "If Johnny White came down, people walking by would see him sitting there, and before you knew it, the bar would be full."

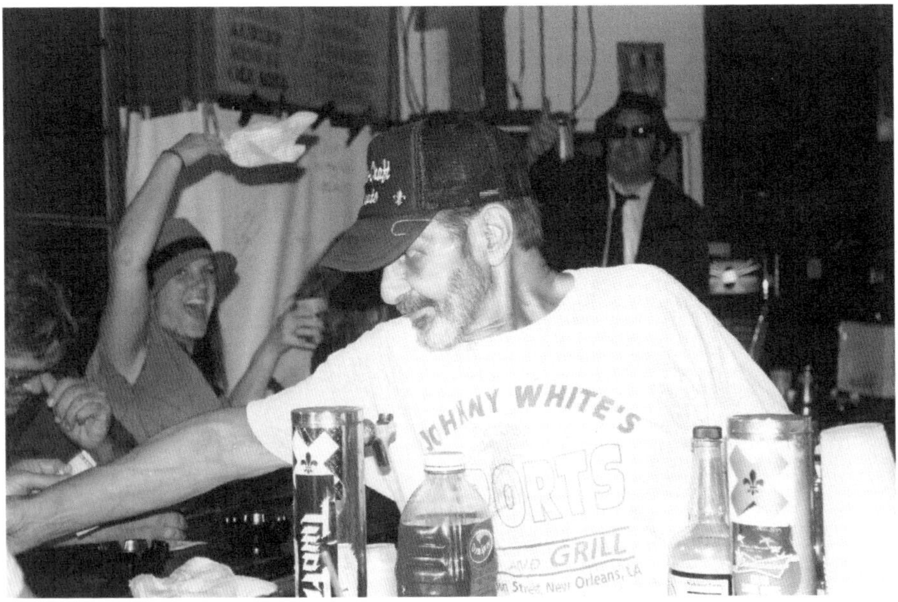

Bartender Byron Penn behind the bar. *Moriah Blue.*

Penn recalls that White's popularity even caught the attention of the celebrity Shirley MacLaine, an actress best known for starring in *Terms of Endearment* and *Steel Magnolias*. Penn said that MacLaine came into the original Johnny White's, on St. Peter, with attitude: "So where is this Johnny White everyone is talking about?" Apparently, White came down from his apartment above the bar and the two went out to dinner.

White purchased the building that would become Johnny White's Sports Bar at the corner of Orleans, expecting Bourbon Street to grow farther down toward Esplanade. At the time business stopped at St. Peter, and anything beyond that was dark at night. That's when his three friends approached him: J.D. Landrum, Tom Hill and Terry France. France was a silent partner, while Landrum and Hill both put elbow grease in getting the bar ready for business. Hill built the actual bar from scratch, and both Landrum and Hill took bar shifts as well. They got local artist Richard from Austin to do extensive sports murals on the walls, which gave the bar an immediate personality. Several of the murals were eventually covered by liquor shelves, but every wall in the tiny establishment was covered with art. Even the ceiling featured a painted baseball diamond. Local artist Charlie Ward did a remarkable mural of jazz and blues musicians that framed the jukebox.

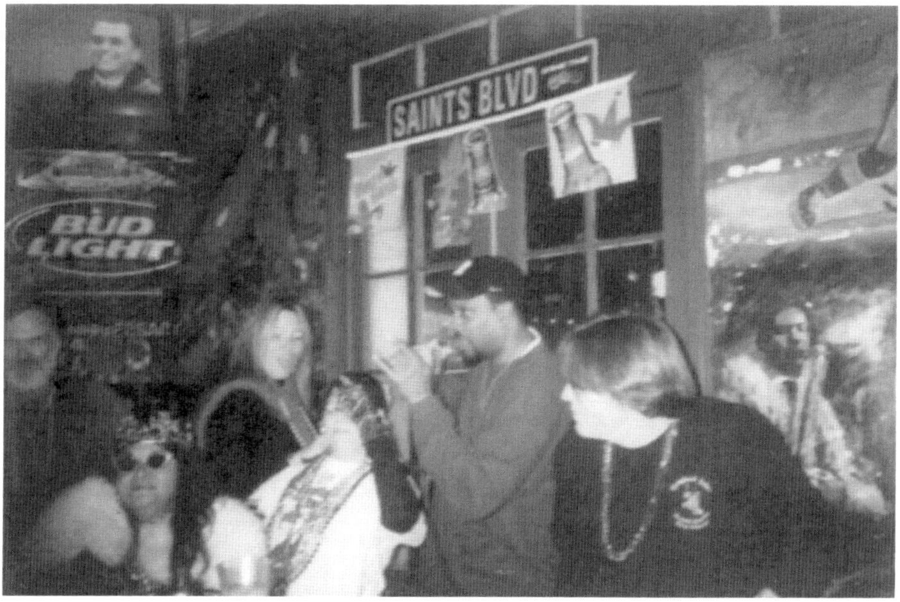

Artwork around the jukebox by Charlie Ward. *Byron Penn.*

Johnny White's name helped the new owners get both their business license and their customers, and the bar quickly became the only locals' bar on Bourbon. The last time there was what would be considered a locals' bar on the touristy Bourbon Street would have been prior to 1964, a bar/restaurant known as the Bourbon House, located on the corner of St. Peter and Bourbon. The newspaper article on the Bourbon House's closing was almost identical to the one that appeared when Johnny White's finally lost its lease more than fifty years later. The Bourbon House also closed due to losing its lease, and its customers also mourned the bar with a mock funeral celebration, complete with a jazz second line.

So, what is it about these unusual bars that have customers mourning their closures as they would the death of a close friend? Is it the colorful customers who frequent the bars that make them so unique, or is it something more? Perhaps centuries of French Quarter history in the location itself contribute to the establishment's unusual personality.

The 1700s were an exciting time when explorers were traveling into unknown territory, discovering different climates and landscapes; they were reeling with the thrill of claiming land for their leaders. New Orleans was a clean slate and brought with it much opportunity. With the Mississippi River allowing passage for trade, it quickly became an important port.

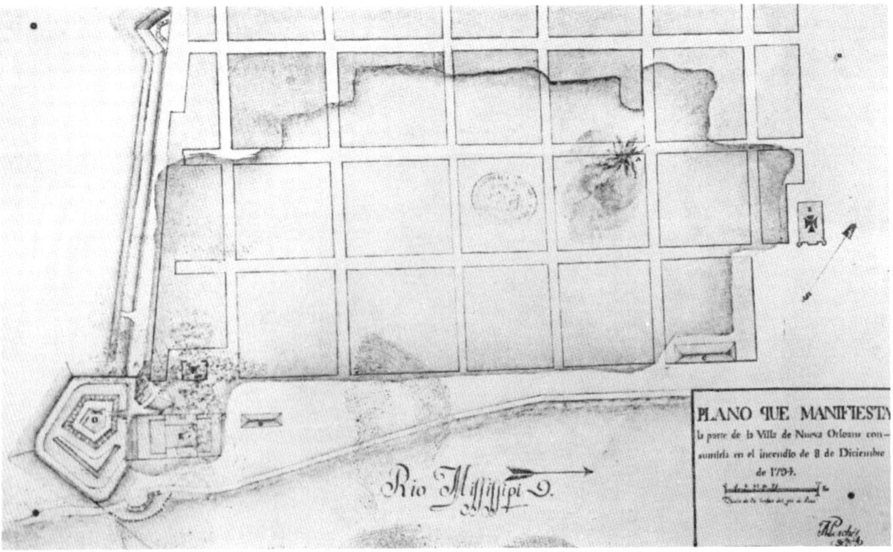

Plans for young New Orleans. *The Collins C. Diboll Vieux Carré Digital Survey at the historic New Orleans Collection, courtesy of Archivo General de Indias (Seville, Spain).*

In 1821, the entire block of Bourbon, from St. Peter to Orleans—including the historic building where Johnny White's Sports Bar would come to stand—was earmarked to house city court buildings:

> *To Architects and Undertakers…informs those persons who wish to undertake the same that the plans adopted for the erection of said Building on the lot fronting on Bourbon, Orleans and St. Peter Streets, are deposited at the office of Mr. Cruzat, Treasurer of this parish. (For the construction of Building to be erected for the accommodation of the Courts of Justice in the City of New Orleans). Sept. 4, 1821*

How different Bourbon Street might have become with the city's governing buildings erected smack in the middle, just behind the Cathedral on Royal. However, that plan never materialized. Not long after, the land was sold, and the building on the corner of Bourbon and Orleans became commercial space, known at the time as "ordinaries."

The first business at this location was a coffee house in 1822. Artists' Coffee House was owned by John Toussaint. Then the space became Café de Foi, which opened on October 2, 1824. On November 7, 1830, yet another coffee house took its place, the Paris Coffee House.

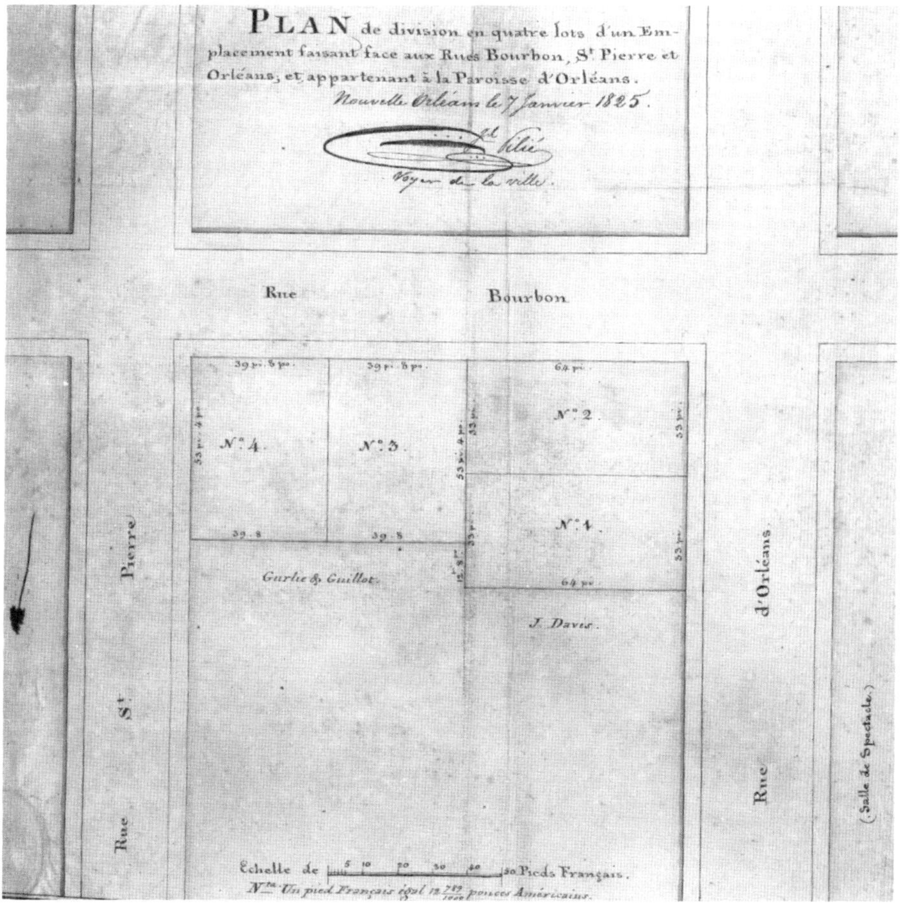

The lots on Bourbon Street earmarked for court buildings. *The Collins C. Diboll Vieux Carré Digital Survey at The historic New Orleans Collection, courtesy of Clerk of Civil District Court, Notarial Archives Division, New Orleans LA, N-2056.*

Paris Coffee House—Notice.

The Subscribers…their Eating House will be open once more prepared to receive customers on Sunday next (Nov.) 7th inst. They have also fixed in such a manner that house that there exists an avenue wherein ladies may be let into the establishment without being seen by the people in Orleans street…M.S. CHAPUS & ANDRE.

Good ladies were not to be seen entering an establishment such as this from the church property, so a separate entrance was arranged for them from the Bourbon Street side, to help protect their reputations.

However, that café didn't last long; just a year later, in November 1831, Café De Paris opened in its place. The city's record then shows several transfers throughout the years without mentioning the type of business that may have existed there, until January 1921, when it was purchased by Paul Joseph Scibetta and Vincent Scibetta, who opened Scibetta's Restaurant, which also maintained a ladies' entrance.

The corner building later became apartments, and it was purchased by Johnny White in 1988 and would house three of the Johnny White establishments: Johnny White's Sports Bar, which is now Johnny White's Corner Pub; Johnny White's Hole in the Wall; and Johnny White's Bar and Grill, located on the second floor with the wraparound balcony overlooking Bourbon and Orleans.

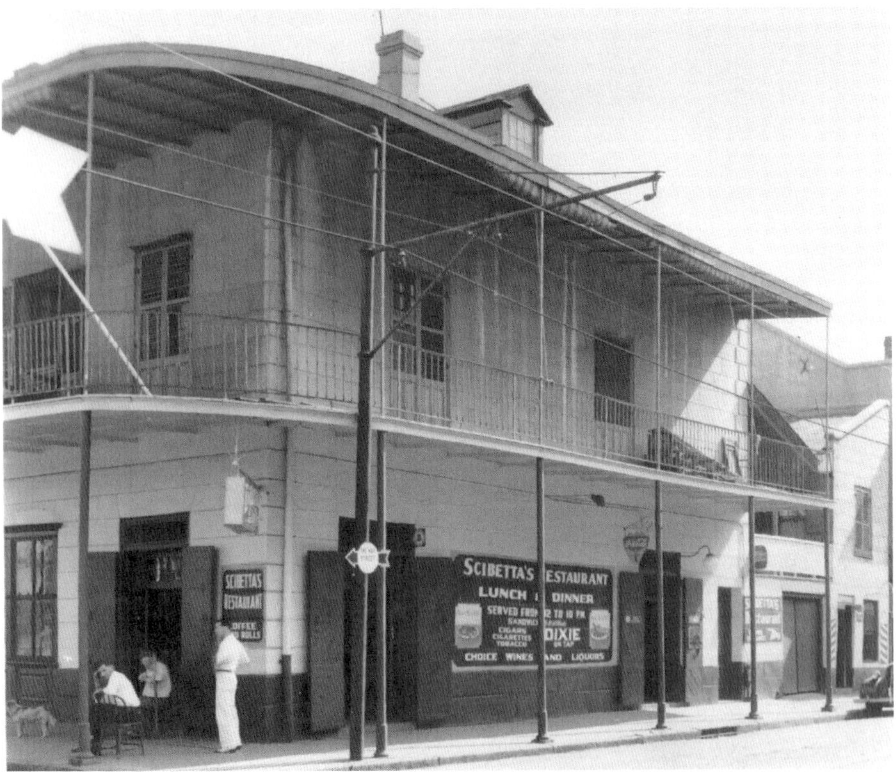

Scibetta's Restaurant. *The Collins C. Diboll Vieux Carré Digital Survey at the historic New Orleans Collection, courtesy of the Louisiana State Museum, 2-060-015.*

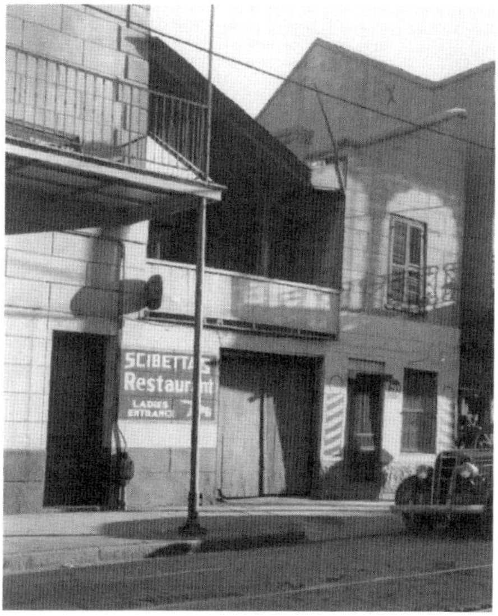

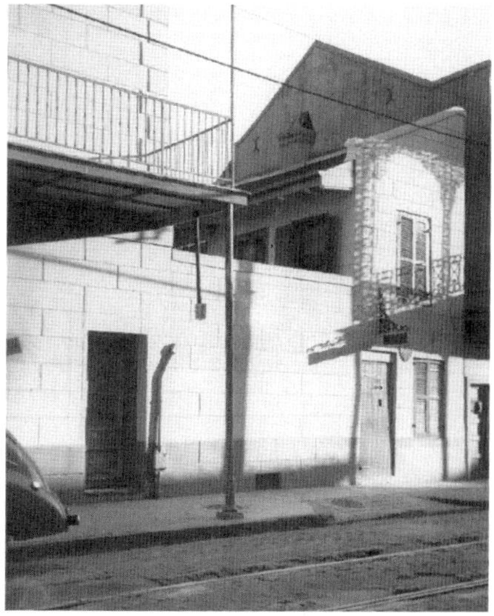

Left: Scibetta's ladies' entrance. *The Collins C. Diboll Vieux Carré Digital Survey at the historic New Orleans Collection, courtesy of the Vieux Carré Commission, 2-060-016.*

Right: 718 Bourbon, before the hole was added for "The Hole in the Wall." *The Collins C. Diboll Vieux Carré Digital Survey at the historic New Orleans Collection, courtesy of the Vieux Carré Commission, 2-060-017.*

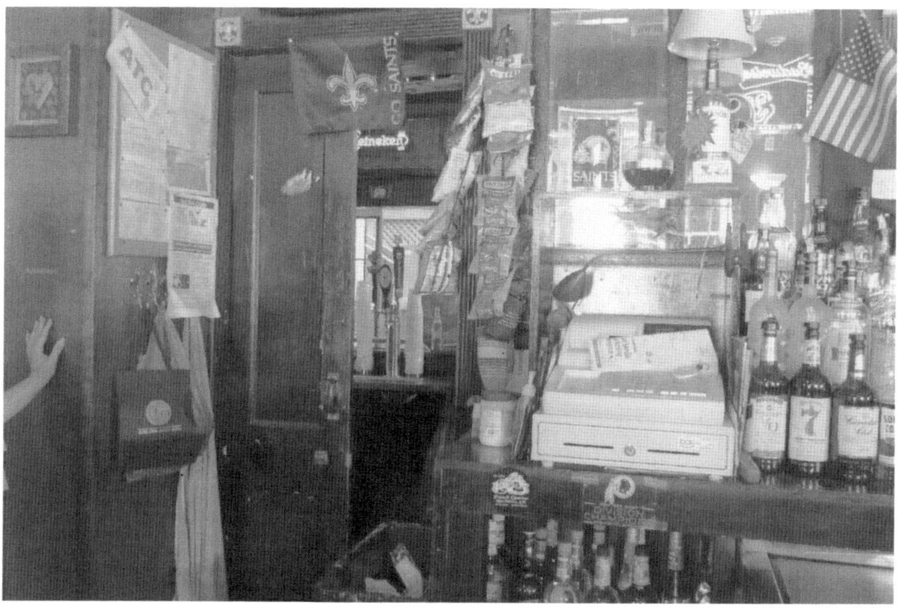

The sliding door between the two bars; it is functional to this day. *Author's collection.*

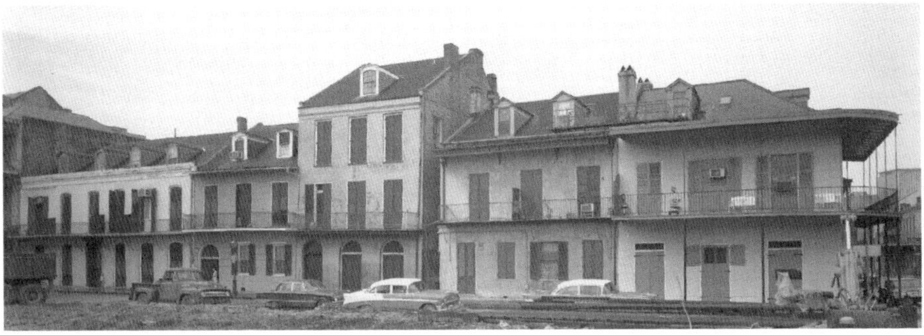

720 Bourbon, before the Bourbon Orleans Hotel was erected. *The Collins C. Diboll Vieux Carré Digital Survey at the historic New Orleans Collection, N-2922D.*

The Hole in the Wall was originally just a beer stand, an actual hole in the wall. The wall was broken in to secure an entrance and small space that became a beer stand for the Whites and later expanded as an actual bar with a sliding door opening to Johnny White's Sports Bar. The door between the two bars is still in place and functional to this day.

Johnny White's Sports Bar, from its inception, came with personality. The owners, bartenders and customers continued to embellish this personality until the day the bar that never closed had to lock its doors.

2

Johnny White's as a Destination

As pioneers on a corner of Bourbon that was far from the excitement of clubs and businesses closer to Canal Street, the new owners of Johnny White's spent 1989 focused on building the bar and ordering liquor to begin their new venture. In walked Susie Hood Kates, a transplant bartender from Arkansas innocently looking for a drink. It was Labor Day weekend, and a large ship, full of sailors ready for a few days of adventure and drinking, happened to dock in New Orleans. Even though the bar was still in the construction phase, J.D. saw opportunity. An influx of sailors was a chance to make money that could not be passed up. He snagged Susie as Johnny White's first bartender, used one of the saw horses to create a makeshift bar and brought in a cooler to hold ice and beer. J.D.'s hustle proved successful, and Susie served many a sailor that day. "For several years, J.D. knew me only as 'Little Girl,'" said Susie. "But he employed me several times over the years and eventually learned my name." It was with this quirky beginning that the bar got its start and set the stage for so many unique experiences along its twenty-three-year journey.

The comfy atmosphere of J.W.'s and the laissez-faire attitude of New Orleans fostered an exuberant and free attitude in its patrons, locals and tourists alike. The bar soon became known for women often stripping down to nothing at all and dancing. Not long after opening the bar, J.D. was approached by a gentleman from Colorado who suggested the then-novel idea of filming the wild women who drank and danced on the bar at the popular Bourbon Street location. Filmed nearly a decade before the

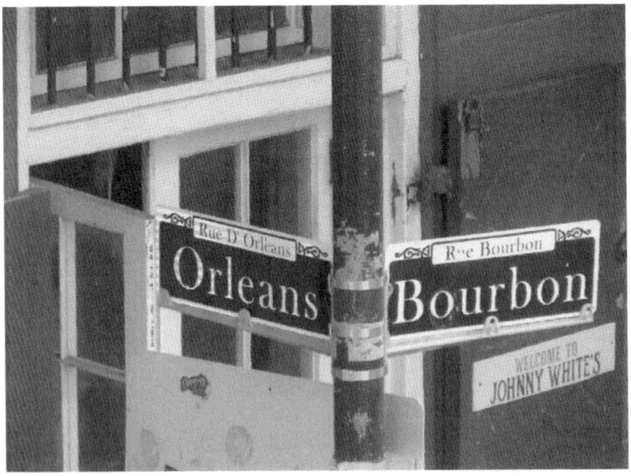

Left: The street sign just outside of the bar. *Author's collection.*

Below: The sports bar's first bartender, Susie Hood Kates. *Author's collection.*

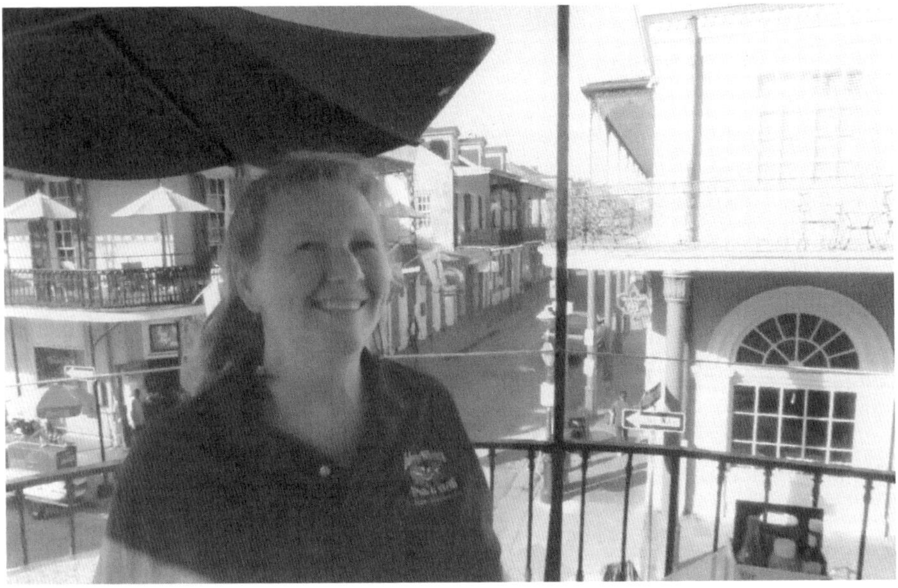

notorious *Girls Gone Wild* series, which began in 1997, these Mardi Gras videos epitomized the fun and debauchery of the French Quarter party scene and put J.W.'s on the map. J.W.'s had a way of making all feel at home, footloose and fancy free, and they quickly lost their inhibitions for the camera. Many women featured on the videos even purchased copies as mementos.

The video producer would show up for Mardi Gras and film the craziness at the bar, and then J.D. would buy the VHS tapes from him to show on the TV screens throughout the year to help make a name for the bar and to promote tape sales. There are many locals who made their Mardi Gras video debuts on one of the early tapes. Some say so proudly; some admit to it with a bit of chagrin.

These videos became so popular that for many years, Johnny White's Sports Bar was known as "the bar with the Mardi Gras videos." It was *Girls Gone Wild* before its time. The videos brought with them the feel of what people who visited Bourbon Street wanted. They wanted the freedom of the city's Storyville past—the decadent, anything-goes-here mentality. In this case, what happened in New Orleans didn't stay in New Orleans. Rather, customers proudly purchased the tapes to share with their friends at home.

When I started working at J.W.'s in March 2002, almost daily, a tourist would ask if we still sold the videos. At the time, we had a nice supply, but apparently sales were nowhere near what they were a few years before that. The novelty was not as great as it was when television was still more censored. Seeing girls freely flaunt their breasts was risqué and very New Orleans. Upon my arrival at the bar, we only showed the videos upon request, although we generally still kept them on twenty-four hours a day during the Mardi Gras season. I found that during Mardi Gras, the videos added to the general gluttonous feel that the festival encouraged. However, after the season, on slow days or nights, some of the other female bartenders and I felt it was a bit uncomfortable to play the video for one patron if they requested it. Being a woman behind the bar and having naked women dancing behind us on the screen had the customers looking at us differently, and little by little, the videos were played less and less.

After the success of *Girls Gone Wild* and other similar shows hitting the television networks, the producer of Johnny White's videos no longer saw a market for producing material specifically for the bar. With that, the few VHS videos that were left became obsolete, as we replaced our televisions with flat screen versions and our VCR recorders with DVD players.

Although the videos eventually fell into disuse, the ahead-of-its-time idea, coupled with the fact that J.W.'s was the only twenty-four-hour bar on Bourbon, really made the little bar a destination. It was the first unique marketing practice that put J.W.'s on the map.

The bar's hours of operation turned it into a locals' bar and a place that tourists felt at home when they just didn't want to go home yet. Many times, a tourist's wife would be across the street at the Bourbon Orleans Hotel, already in bed sound asleep, and here came the husband, not wanting his night to end. Tourists loved the novelty of being able to spend their night at a twenty-four-hour bar, chatting and laughing with locals.

THE LIQUOR ROOM HOTEL

J.D., having had some tough times in life himself, was understanding and tolerant of people who had hit a bad patch. The bar had bathrooms and a liquor/ice room upstairs. The liquor room was fairly small. You had to go up a few stairs from the ice machine. On your right were the plastic cups, and straight ahead were several shelves stocked with various types of liquor. It wasn't a place you wanted to spend much time. However, there was just enough room in front of the liquor shelves to spread out a coat, use a backpack as a pillow, and get some shut-eye—an attractive option for those with nowhere else to stay. The liquor room's proximity to the bathroom made it easy to freshen up before heading back out to the bar, so, on many occasions, regulars—and sometimes even J.W.'s employees—would take advantage of the privacy of this unique situation.

When I started working there, Sam, an older black man who would get us ice during our shift for tips, had moved into the liquor room on a nightly basis. He worked getting ice until it was time to check in for the night. He always asked if we needed one more bucket before he turned in. Then he would go upstairs and ask to be locked in for the night. The door had a padlock on the outside, and Sam didn't want to be bothered by strangers checking to see where the door might lead. This went on for months, maybe even a year. We would go in throughout the night and get more ice, and the first action on the morning shift would be to unlock the room and let Sam come down to the bar. Sam eventually moved out of the Quarter, and J.W.'s liquor room was once again available to those without a place to stay for the night.

The liquor room was a haven for many French Quarter locals who needed a break and a safe place to rest for just enough time to get back on their feet. No one in the bar looked down on these individuals, rather, the people of J.W.'s, whether they cared for the person or not, were genuinely pleased when they checked out of the liquor room to move on to the next chapter in their lives. While we all knew it was an unconventional situation, and a bit crazy, it seemed kind. It came from the heart, and that was the spirit of Johnny White's—welcoming, hilarious, forgiving and unique.

3

The Haunting of Johnny White's

People often say the French Quarter is haunted because it's so old. The Quarter's age cannot be the only factor behind its ghostly notoriety, as in the grand scheme of things, the city is very young. Nonetheless, most buildings in the French Quarter do seem to have spirits that cling to them. Some of the spirits may have experienced a tragic death, either don't know or don't want to believe that they have passed, or perhaps they are looking for answers or maybe even revenge. Or maybe when the French Quarter of New Orleans grabs your heart, your soul chooses to linger among the Spanish lace, brick and slate so adored during life.

Unsurprisingly, for a place that fully embraced the quirks and spirit of New Orleans, Johnny White's had its share of ghosts, too. Many people over the years have talked about the woman in the blue dress upstairs at the bar. The dress was old and Victorian in style, floor-length, like the kind you might see at costume balls now. Most people who saw the ghost would catch only a glimpse of her at the top of the stairs, and then she would vanish. Strangely, tourists would often mention seeing her to the staff, although they could not have heard about this resident spirit before their sighting. The most vivid story of the woman up the stairs came from Johnny White's janitor Paul. Paul started his shift early, sometimes before the morning shift even started. The graveyard drinkers were still nursing their drinks, waiting for a nudge to send them home. Paul's arrival, on many days, was that nudge. He would ask one side of the bar to temporarily vacate their stools so he could pull them away from the bar and mop the floor. Then he would do the other side of the bar. For many, this was just the inspiration required to stay on their feet and walk out the bar.

On one such morning, there were many people left in the bar playing the jukebox, laughing, drinking and vested in their real estate. Paul, having just woken up, wasn't in the mood to tackle the job of raising the complacent. He instead decided to clean the upstairs bathrooms first. The door to the ladies' room was a little ajar, and when he went to push it open, a woman's voice shouted "Oh!" and someone quickly pushed against the door from the other side until it caught the latch and closed. Paul apologized and leaned back against the wall on the landing to wait for the woman to exit. He waited quite some time and finally decided to go downstairs and ask Marcie, the bartender on duty, if she had any idea who was in the restroom. Marcie looked around and told him everyone was accounted for; she had no idea who could be in the ladies' room. Paul went back upstairs and found the door wide open with no one in sight. There was only one way down the stairs, so Paul would have seen anyone exit. It was a mystery that was never solved, and it gave Paul an eerie feeling. Several people claim to have seen the woman in the blue dress at the top of the stairs, usually in the early morning hours. Perhaps she was an original customer of the Artists' Coffee House in the 1820s and had enjoyed her time in the building as much as we all did so many years later.

The regulars at Johnny White's would sometimes talk about how after we were all dead and gone we would be right back at Johnny White's, playing the jukebox, dancing, drinking and laughing with our friends who had become more like family. Unfortunately, over the years, we have lost several bartenders and regulars, but we have pictured them all still socializing in the little bar that they called home. While the bar may no longer be there, its spirit certainly carries on, and it is easy to visualize our little bar having its own place in heaven.

4

True Crimes

The French Quarter is very welcoming if you intend to reinvent yourself or disappear. It is not uncommon to get hired on the spot, without even offering your full name. Those who live in the Quarter often joke about not knowing one another's last names. In fact, anywhere from 25 to 50 percent of the regulars who cross your path in the Quarter go by a nickname—adding to that quirky flavor of the city—and it simply isn't questioned. Being so easy to blend in makes the neighborhood a desirable location for those on the lam.

I remember J.D telling me early on to not put too much stock in anyone's "story," as most are either embellished a bit or entirely made up. "You can come to New Orleans and be whoever you want to be," he said. While that's really a beautiful thing, it also leads to one hobnobbing with criminals and even murderers.

My first month in New Orleans, late 2001, the French Quarter was abuzz with news that someone had "blown their head off at Johnny White's," in this case, the original Johnny White's on St. Peter Street. Apparently, a man in his late forties came in with a briefcase, sat down and solemnly drank a beer while staring at his cellphone. He had several beers, and his isolated behavior made him stand out from the crowd. Eventually, he got up, leaving his briefcase on the floor and his beer and phone on the bar and went the bathroom. Then came the sound of a gunshot. Lulu, the bartender at the time, said the FBI was at the scene in no time. They pried open the briefcase and found multiple IDs for the man, who was running from his past of child molesting. Over the years, there were many stories of people with whom we socialized at J.W.'s who were somehow running from the law. It was always a little shocking to hear but also easily plausible.

Another man arrived in town and quickly obtained the job of manager at a very nice restaurant on Decatur Street, the Italian Barrel. One of our regulars worked for him, and he would often come in and join her at the bar. Yet he never came in on his own. He rode a bicycle, and I remember that he would pull up on his bike, poke his head in, and, if he didn't see his employee in the bar, ride off. My intuition kicked in, and I knew something about him was off, but I didn't think it was anything devious. Rather, I thought he was just strange and was perhaps trying to date my friend. He only drank White Russians when he came in, and I honestly can't explain it, but he very much rubbed me the wrong way. One day, he ordered a rum and Diet Coke. I thought it was odd, only because it was the first time he had ordered anything but a White Russian. It is something that bartenders notice.

Not long after that, he arrived with our regular to enjoy a few cocktails. Remembering that the last drink he ordered from me was a rum and Coke, I decided to ask him if he would like one. His reaction was quite unusual. Looking at me as if I were insane, he said sternly, "I only drink White Russians!"

"No, you don't," I thought to myself, but I decided to let it go and turned to make his drink.

Well, not two weeks later, the television was turned to the news, and there he was—a big mug shot of our "friend." Our jaws all dropped, but I had an aha moment. Turns out he was on *America's Most Wanted* for child molestation. I don't recall all the details, but he eventually turned himself in in California. After the news came out, several bartenders from other bars happened to be visiting me at J.W.'s. We were talking about this guy and how we had our suspicions about him. I mentioned my story about the White Russians, and the other three bartenders' faces went white. It turned out that in one of the bars, he only drank screwdrivers, rum and Diet Cokes in the other, and I don't recall what he drank in the fourth bar. It gave me chills, because he was most likely trying to set up some kind of an alibi or misdirection for himself. If someone came looking for him, and they said, "You know, the guy who only drinks screwdrivers," I would have said, "Oh, no, can't be the same guy." Bartenders do remember these things, and he knew it.

In the French Quarter, we socialize with people from all walks of life, and because the people at Johnny White's were so nonjudgmental, we have all rubbed elbows with thieves, criminals and even murders. Many shades of gray existed between the black and white at J.W.'s. Johnny White's was a place where you could get a second chance; all you had to do was sincerely want it. On more than one occasion, we were let down by someone we trusted, but for every one of those, there were two stories of people succeeding and impressing us with their endeavors.

5

The Graveyard Shift

When I first began working at the bar, I was pleased and honored to be given the graveyard shift, as any shift at J.W.'s was coveted. I had been a customer there for a couple of months, so I had an idea of what to expect. During any graveyard shift, especially in the French Quarter, you were sure to experience colorful situations with which nothing else could ever compare. Some might hear our stories and wonder why we would put ourselves in such a position. For me, it was both enlightening and entertaining. I believe that our unusual situation of being a locals' bar on Bourbon Street created the most colorful stories one could imagine. However, I learned from some of our regulars that the French Quarter was definitely a strange animal that welcomed and was tolerant of behavior that would surely be shunned almost everywhere else.

On my first few nights of tending bar, I was on my best behavior. I don't think I even had a drink until my shift was over because I was so scared of making a mistake. It's hard to even think back that far anymore.

One night, a burly guy over six feet tall with a full gray beard and ponytail sat down at the bar. In a husky voice, he ordered a rum and Coke as if he owned the place. Then *it* happened—my first mistake. Out of habit, I poured him a well rum and Diet Coke. Luckily, I noticed the error right away, my finger still on the diet button. "Oops, I made it diet," I said.

"Oh, no, that won't do darling," he replied as he hacked on his cigarette.

I was looking forward to drinking this mistake. I set it aside and poured the old guy another. He introduced himself as Ron. The most difficult

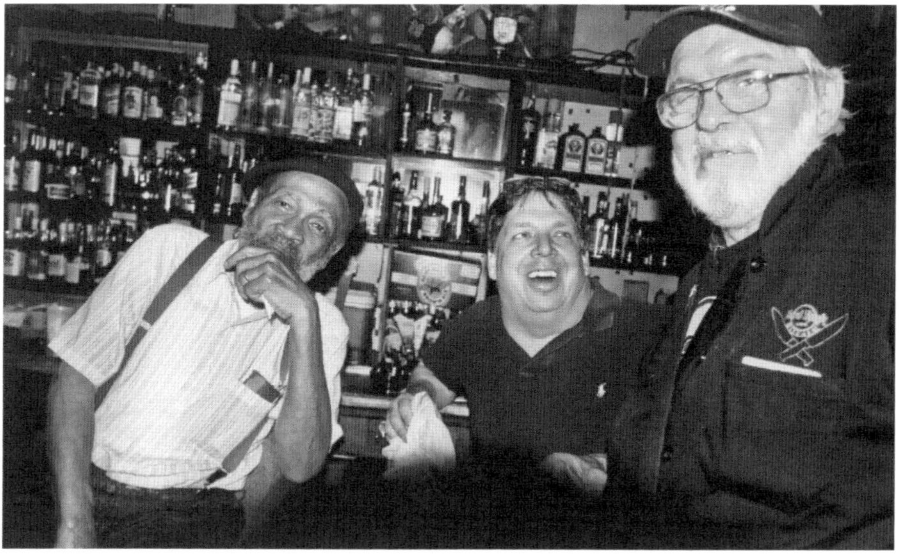

Charlie Sims (*left*) pictured with regulars John Fox (*middle*) and Ron Herring. *Moriah Blue.*

part about working at this bar in the beginning was deciphering who was a regular customer and who was just a walk-in off Bourbon Street. When new customers came in, I usually waited them out a minute to see what colorful introduction they would make to me. The more colorful the introduction, the more regular they were. We had two sets of prices, as most bars here do: one for customers and one for regulars. I quickly learned it was better to figure it out on my own or the lectures came flying.

After a brief conversation with Ron, I deduced that he was a regular. He tried to make me feel comfortable and told me a bit about himself and his relationship with the bar. He sensed I was a greenhorn at tending bar, so he asked me to pull up my stool, and my mistake drink, so he could boost my confidence.

"I've been around here a long time," he lectured. He wanted to seem wiser than he really was. "The thing about the Quarter is, people take you for who you are. Everybody screws up here, and more than once, but no one holds a grudge for long.

"I used to work at a bar around the corner, the graveyard shift, 1:00 a.m. to 8:00 a.m. at that time. Five nights a week. You're gonna see, summertime is slow here. Real slow. So anyway, I was having some cocktails on this summer night, watching some old western on the tube. I hadn't had a customer in about three hours."

He took a long swallow of his drink through the straw. I could tell he was pleased to have my attention. I could picture Ron, relaxed behind the bar with a rum and Coke, manning his post. Harry's is a cozy neighborhood bar on Chartres Street. It has a nice feel about it, with a fireplace in the corner, a jukebox with a well-thought-out collection of both local and mainstream tunes and a great crowd of regulars.

Ron was a good storyteller if you had the time. He enjoyed recollecting every detail of a moment, which I have to admit helped paint a picture. He explained that he had been at the bar for hours, first as a customer, and later starting his shift behind the bar. Few customers came through the door that evening, and the ones who did hadn't stayed long. It made for a long, drawn-out evening for Ron, and his westerns weren't keeping him entertained on this night. So, he poured himself up some drinks.

It started innocently enough. However, before he knew it, Ron was three sheets to the wind and still bored.

"Man, I finally had to use the pisser," he grinned. "So, I came around the bar and went to the john. I was so far gone on rum and boredom, when I came back, I pulled up a stool at the bar and waited for the damn bartender to get back."

And there he waited a good while, cursing whoever it was who wasn't at their post, not realizing in his drunken stupor that "I was waiting on my own stupid ass," he admitted.

Ron had gotten so fed up waiting for the bartender, he decided he'd had enough to drink and left the bar, went home and slept it off. Eventually, a regular, Terry Foley, the man who had rented me my apartment, came in and found the bar empty, called the owner to come down and held post until she arrived. No harm, no foul.

"I got fired, but that's really beside the point," Ron explained. "What I'm trying to tell you is, it's all water under the bridge. I'm not saying people don't still talk about that little episode, but they don't fault me for it. You see what I'm saying?"

I made a mental note at that moment that if I did open my nightclub, Ron wouldn't be working there, but he was so genuine and self-confident I couldn't help but like him. I also promised myself that I would never drink so many mistakes that I would ever find myself on the other side of the bar, waiting for a cocktail, during my shift.

On one of my first nights behind the bar, Ron's story was a great introduction to what was to lie ahead. I have been in other local bars on various occasions and overheard someone retelling a version of Ron's story to a friend or customer. If it's appropriate, I will interject and correct them so they get it right, only because the truth in this case is more interesting than the version they happen to be telling. Sometimes I just sit back and listen and smile to myself.

Ron is just one of those French Quarter characters who will have stories of them retold again and again over time. It's what makes the French Quarter a great place for writers. It's these unusual personages who live and work in the French Quarter that create the unique atmosphere so many come here to enjoy.

Bourbon Street Bartenders

They say if you visit a graveyard late at night on a day when new graves have been filled, you will see a green mist, known as "the green hue," floating above the ground. There's a simple explanation, really. The bodies, beginning their decomposition, emit vapors that creep to the surface, creating this eerie effect. In fact, one of our customers told me he used to dig graves for extra money while he was in high school. He said he would often take girls up to the graveyard at night when this green fog would float about and appear to creep toward them. He had already filled their heads with notions that perhaps ghouls might rise out of the mist. Then he could be their protector.

Well, my graveyard shifts also had a misty green hue—only it was a layer of green goop on Bourbon Street that was created from the oodles of spilt

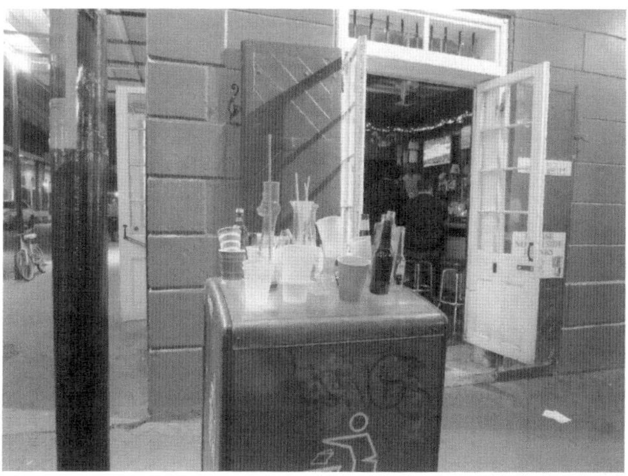

The trashcan just outside of Johnny White's, set up for Bourbon Street Bartenders to start mixing. *Author's collection.*

and often regurgitated Hand Grenades, a melon green–colored specialty drink sold at the popular Tropical Isle bars. And our ghouls were drunks who had fallen onto the street to nap. They would rise like the living dead, stumbling about picking up leftover cups and containers that might have a taste of some liquor left.

During my graveyard shift, we would often watch from the bar windows as these truly zombie-like drunks sometimes created their own concoctions from the rest of other people's drinks. We coined them "Bourbon Street Bartenders." Drunk, homeless zombies pouring a variety of liquor into one suicide elixir, they would proudly savor these concoctions for hours as they roamed the French Quarter greeting one another.

In the safety of Johnny White's, however, the middle of the night and wee hours of the morning were always entertaining. Many times, the bar would be full of actual bartenders who had just ended their shifts and were ready to unwind with a drink. We would watch the goings-on from the window while sharing stories about funny tourists and other unusual things that might have happened to us during our shifts.

6

Ruthie the Duck Lady

While I never met Ruthie the Duck Lady, Ruth Grace Moulon's antics were still in full swing when I arrived in the Quarter. A regular would come into the bar and announce that Ruthie had escaped from her nursing home and was barhopping throughout the Quarter, bumming cigarettes and beer as fast as she could before one of her friends would return her to the home.

Ruthie was a New Orleans native whose mother decided early on that it was in Ruthie's best interest for her to become a French Quarter celebrity. It was her mother who originally gifted Ruthie her first ducks, to help build her French Quarter persona. Ruthie, her brother and their mother lived with the ducks in an apartment on Royal Street. For reasons unknown, Ruthie never went to school. Her schooling consisted of the lessons of life, which, it turned out, she lived to the fullest.

Ruthie was a regular at J.W.'s as well as many other bars throughout the Quarter. In her earlier years, she was famous for riding through the Quarter on roller skates, followed by at least one duck wherever she went. Saying she was rough around the edges would be an understatement. Ruthie had a foul mouth, and to this day when you mention her name, people who knew her well smile and say, "Gimme a cigarette—one for now and one for layda." She would do the same with beer.

Apparently, her reputation preceded her, and if you were in a bar and she appeared, you felt honored to be in her presence. J.W.'s regular Laura Rapp said, "I had heard a lot about her, but when she finally came into the bar

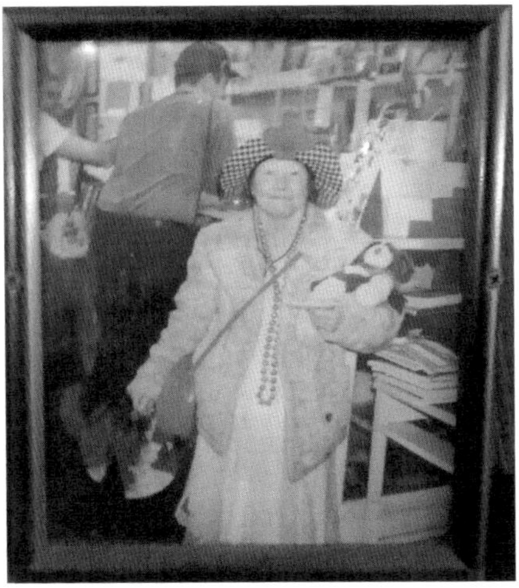

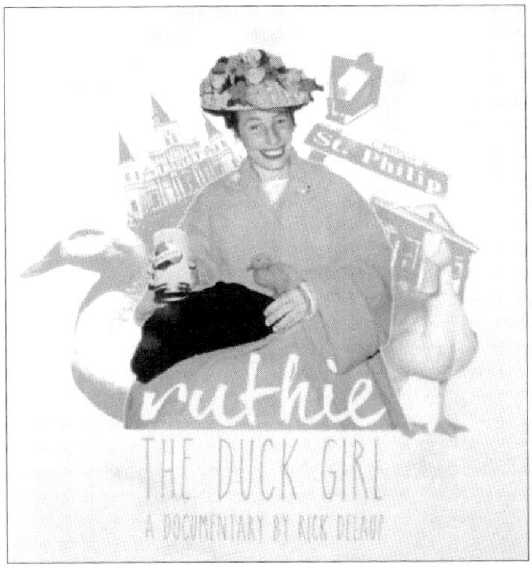

Left: Ruthie the Duck Lady's framed photograph hangs in the original Johnny White's on St. Peter Street. She is pictured wearing a jacket bought for her by Johnny White's wife, Mary Louise Glynn. *Author's collection.*

Right: The DVD cover for the documentary *Ruthie the Duck Girl*, by Rick Delaup. *Author's collection.*

and I got a chance to meet her, she immediately asked me for a cigarette and one for later. I quickly reached into my purse to appease her and was feeling good about donating to this French Quarter character. Then she looked me over and said, "You look like a hussy."

Ruthie was apparently never short of insults, and somehow, it suited her. She lived with her mother and her ducks on Esplanade Street. She was infamous for wearing tattered faux fur coats, one of which was given to her by Mary Louise Glynn White, Johnny White's wife.

Robert C. Adler related a colorful anecdote about the French Quarter's notorious Duck Lady in a November 1974 article for the *Community Standard*:

> *Ruthie the Duck Lady was walking down St. Peter Street with a little black duck waddling behind her. When they reached Bourbon Street she paused, turned to the duck and said, "You wait here." Apparently, the duck did not understand, and, while crossing the street, was run over by a NOPSI bus. A crowd formed around the moosh of feathers. Back marched Ruthie. Shaking a finger at the former duck, she scolded, "I told you to wait (you stupid duck)."*

Ruthie the Duck Girl also is the title of a moving and delightful documentary created by Rick Delaup in 1999, and it is often shown on New Orleans PBS station WYES. Johnny White's Sports Bar regular Lynn Head, who has sadly since passed away, was interviewed throughout the video. At J.W.'s, she is filmed telling a story of when someone came in the sports bar and called Ruthie stupid. Ruthie apparently said, "You think I'm stupid? When was the last time you paid for a beer?" The guy said, "Well, just a few minutes ago." Ruthie replied, "I haven't paid for one in twenty years, and you think I'm stupid."

Eventually, Ruthie traded in her roller skates for shoes without wheels, and much later, her duck was replaced by a stuffed version of her once animated feathered friends, but her personality was the same. "Miss Moulon, a lifelong New Orleanian, became a French Quarter fixture, achieving legendary status in a city that treasures people who live outside the mainstream," wrote John Pope in an article for the *Times Picayune* in 2008. The article was written in Ruthie's honor upon her death on September 22, 2008. She died of mouth cancer at the age of seventy-four.

7

Meeting Tommy Pye

When I started my job at J.W.'s on St. Patrick's Day 2002, I replaced Tommy Pye., a J.W.'s institution. I heard about it for a good long time. Tommy Pye got a job across the street, at the then Trico House, after J.D. fired him and replaced him with me. J.D. had a hard time firing Tommy Pye, but after so many years of tending bar, Tommy was said to be harsh and mean to customers, pushing business away. I'd heard Tommy was a mean old sort who didn't put up with anything. He threw people out before they even made it through the door. He was unapologetically prejudiced, and he thought very little of women.

Then I heard from the same people that he was wonderful. He was a great dancer, and the women he would entertain as customers he would treat like gold. He sounded colorful, and I thought it would be in my best interest to make his acquaintance.

One night before work, I went to see Tommy Pye at the Trico House. I had all kinds of expectations. I thought that once I introduced myself, he would be angry with me and most likely treat me badly. That night, I brought along someone I had just started dating. His name was Steve, and he is now my husband. Steve is a six-foot-six black man. Somehow it hadn't crossed my mind that prejudice was one of Tommy Pye's noted characteristics until we sat down. So now, I was Marita, the woman, the bartender who replaced him, accompanied by her black boyfriend. Yeah, that would go over well.

Tommy was somewhat as I had imagined: crew cut, strong features and definite confidence. However, everything changed when I introduced myself.

A large, genuine smile came across his face. He served Steve and me a couple of drinks and entertained us charmingly. I waved at him now and then when I passed by the Trico House, and he always smiled. I don't know if the change in positions gave him a boost or what, but both Steve and I enjoyed our drink with Tommy Pye. All those who knew him said he had a different take on life since his job change. It might have been the graveyard shift that had him grumpy, or maybe seeing the same people day after day was getting on his nerves. In his new position, he was primarily serving tourists on vacation ready to have fun.

A few years later, news hit the sports bar hard that Tommy Pye had cancer and had only a few short months to live. Well, Tommy took his life's savings and went vacationing—high on the hog. Apparently, he had a grand time and spent most of his fortune. However, when he came back from frolicking in the tropics, he went to visit his doctor. The doctor gleefully informed Tommy that his cancer had cleared, and he was good to go.

Tommy had no option but to start working again, and the gruff personality he had been known for quickly returned. However, the doctor wasn't all that right, and we lost Tommy a few years back now. Tommy had requested that his ashes be spread among a few locations, one of which was Johnny White's Sports Bar. One of our regulars purchased a nice little wooden box with a horse pictured on the front, as Tommy was a big fan of the races. They carefully poured a portion of the ashes in the box, closed it and placed it prominently on the ledge above the front liquor display for all to admire.

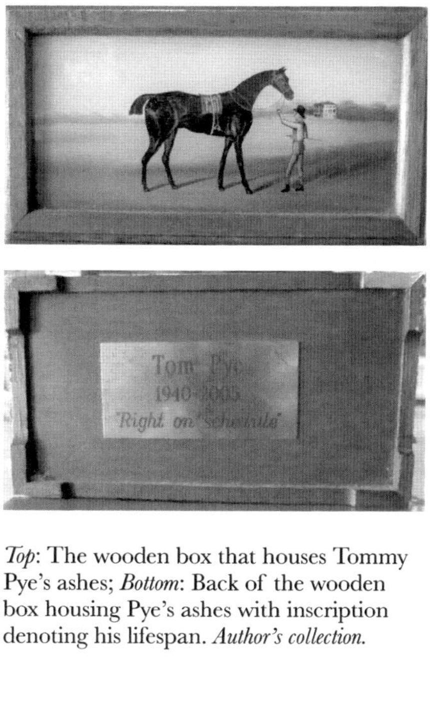

Top: The wooden box that houses Tommy Pye's ashes; *Bottom*: Back of the wooden box housing Pye's ashes with inscription denoting his lifespan. *Author's collection.*

Enter bartender Jennifer S. J.D. didn't always make the most rational choices in hiring bartenders. In fact, many of his decisions were led by his love for the opposite sex. Jennifer was one of J.D.'s hires whom he hoped to woo. However, she was a fun-loving type and, after learning how to tend bar, became important to J.W.'s. She ordered the liquor and was jovial with all the customers. But on one strange day, Jennifer spotted the box. She was excited to see this wooden box with a "horsey" so cutely pictured on the front that she reached for it. It was up a little too high and slipped through her fingers and, oops, hit the bar. The impact forced it open, and Tommy's ashes spewed about. A couple of regulars knew what had just transpired. At first, they were speechless, but it wasn't long before they helped Jennifer gather what they could of the remains and put them back in the tiny box.

Since then, the box has been sealed and, minus the few lost ashes, remained sitting on the ledge above the liquor display until the bar finally closed, at which time it moved to our sister bar MRB's (Mississippi River Bottom). I look at it now and then and remember Tommy Pye.

8
Windex Pete

One of the regulars at J.W.'s graveyard shift was Windex Pete. Pete had his own original French Quarter gig to make money. Instead of being a hustler or street performer, Pete offered a service. He rode his bicycle throughout the French Quarter, armed with a bottle of Windex and a cloth. He would wash shop windows, car windows and your eyeglasses if the opportunity presented itself. Not long ago, he changed his gig and name to Washboard Pete. He is now adorned with a washboard around his neck and can often be seen playing his washboard with a spoon for tourists around the Quarter.

My first introduction to Windex Pete was shortly after I moved to the Quarter in 2001. A good friend of mine, Rob Deters, and his group of friends had coincidentally planned their annual guys' trip to New Orleans during the first week I arrived in the city. Knowing I was new in town, and a bit worried for my safety in the French Quarter, Rob felt a bit protective of me. So, while our group was walking down Pirate's Alley, Rob and another one of the group dragged behind. They had befriended Windex Pete in the alley, and he was kindly trying to give them directions in exchange for a small tip. Pete had one eye that was a bit askew, and he never looked dirty, but he never looked clean. Anyway, apparently, Pete was so charming that night in the alley that my dear, concerned friend Rob felt compelled to pull him aside and have a little talk with him—about me.

You see, as I had just moved to New Orleans and all, Rob just wanted to make sure I had someone looking out for me. Rob decided this man, this

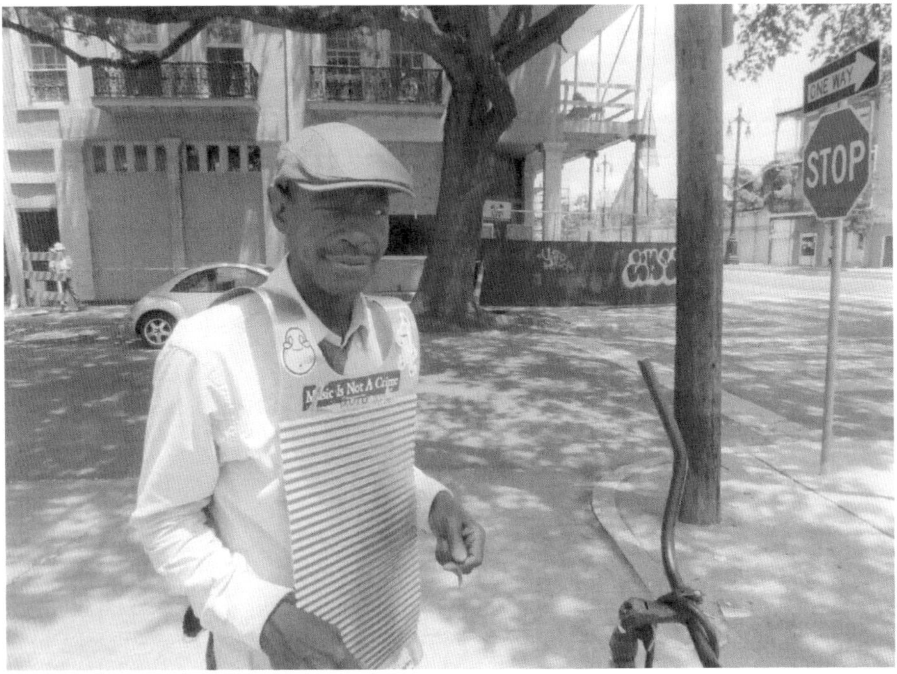

Washboard Pete, formerly Windex Pete. *Author's collection.*

wonderful, helpful man who lingered in the alley giving out directions for tips, would be just the guy to make sure nothing bad happened to me.

I turned around to look for Rob, just as I saw him giving some money to Pete. They sped up a bit to catch up with us, and Rob introduced me to Windex. Windex then winked at Rob, and they bid each other goodbye.

Well, don't you know, Windex Pete took his job seriously. No matter where I went, every time I turned around, out of nowhere, there was Windex Pete. At first, I didn't realize what was going on. However, every time Windex would just happen to be there, he would always say, "Hey remember me? Just making sure you're okay." It was so creepy having this unusual guy on a bike with a Windex bottle and paper towels following me throughout the Quarter—daily.

This went on consistently for several weeks and off and on for about a year—until one day, we met inside of Johnny White's. Windex was enjoying a beer, and I started to turn around and walk out, but I guess I'd finally had enough. I walked over to him and said, "Windex—you have got to stop following me everywhere."

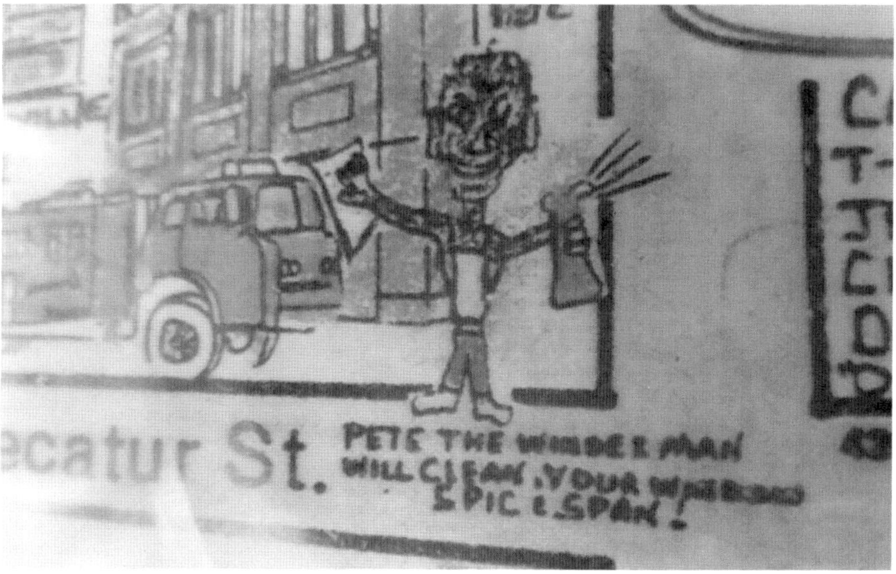

Caricature of Windex Pete featured on a New Orleans promotional street map. *Author's collection.*

He replied, "But I promised. You don't understand, I promised your friend I'd look out for you!" That's when it hit me that this hadn't just been Windex randomly following me around. It was because of Rob. Well, I explained to Pete that I was just fine on my own now. I told him I appreciated it, but I seriously couldn't take being followed anymore. I could tell Pete sincerely felt uncomfortable giving up his post, but he agreed to set me free.

Windex Pete became a regular at the graveyard shift of Johnny White's after that, and now and then he would be eighty-sixed for doing something uncalled for. Many times he just didn't know when to leave, to the point of annoying tourists, so banning him from the bar for a bit would calm him down until he was welcome back. Overall, he was liked by our little family, and I always have a smile for Pete when I see him. Rob certainly got his money's worth.

A few years back, there was a wave of concern at the news that Pete had been shot. No one knew the whole story, but we got word that it wasn't fatal. Before we knew it, Pete was back on his bike.

I later found out that Pete was quite a well-known French Quarter character. He was even featured on a map of French Quarter businesses and interesting tourist information that was sold and circulated throughout the Quarter.

9

I Bought the T-Shirt

A little over one year after I moved to New Orleans, I opened my little vampire-themed shop, Boutique du Vampyre, just three doors down from Johnny White's on Orleans. It was very convenient. When I tended bar at Johnny White's, my boyfriend Steve would man the shop. Occasionally, I would send customers down to him to increase our chances of sales. My friend Anne also agreed to work for us, and I did the same with her. Many times, I would send the customers along with a drink for either Steve or Anne. Customers got a kick out of the gesture, carrying a drink out of the bar and down the street, something they would never be able to do wherever they were from.

Anne happened to be working at the boutique on my favorite day of the year, April Fools' Day. I had resided in New Orleans for only a short time, so no one was on to me yet. These days, I must be extra clever, as all those around me have learned to be on guard for pranks.

I was drinking a mistake when a very nice man from New York, John, entered the bar. We struck up a conversation, and all the while, he never expected that I was secretly sizing him up to help me with an April Fools' joke on Anne at my shop. John was just finishing telling me that he lived in New York but frequently visited New Orleans and that he might just get a little second home in the city. I noticed his expression change a little as he faded off his last few words; he had noticed a little gleam in my eye and an inquisitive look on my face. He tilted his head, as if to ask, "What's up?"

"How are you at acting?" I could see it was not at all what he had expected.

"Oh, I don't know. I've never really tried." And with that, New York John became my protégé.

I had painted two black-and-white paintings in oil on wood as decoration for my shop. Wood made a unique canvas, as it gave an unusual texture to the paintings, with a very pleasing outcome. One was a vampire from the back disappearing into a French Quarter alleyway. The other was of Elizabeth Bathory, the Hungarian countess, toasting with a glass of blood. The images appeared somewhat three-dimensional, and I decided they would be a part of the shop and not for sale. When we opened, we had very few products. We had handmade candles, a few wine accessories, some T-shirts with our logo on them and Vamp n.r.g. drink. That was it. I really had no idea how to run a boutique. Our location was bad, our product mix was insufficient and the economy in New Orleans had slumped dramatically in the wake of 9/11.

In other words, we badly needed money. However, I had made it very clear to both Steve and Anne that these two particular paintings were to be a part of the shop, and under no circumstances were they to be sold. I had to be stern about it because Steve was a very good salesman, and he sold everything. One time, someone brought me a pair of Mardi Gras beads that were German-themed, with cool beer steins attached. I set them on my desk, went to the back to use the bathroom, and when I came back, they were gone. Perplexed, I asked Steve what had happened to my beads. "I sold them." He said proudly, "Woman, I got nine dollars for them." I really couldn't argue.

So, instilling the fear of God in Steve if he sold my paintings was the only way to keep them as part of the décor of the shop. Anne was an innocent bystander, and witnessing my rantings to Steve about the paintings most likely made them seem even more important to her. She got the message.

So, on this lovely April Fools' Day, I thought it would be fun to send John down to the shop as nothing more than a tourist/art buyer. I had told him some details about the paintings so that John would appear to be a true appreciator of my art. Anne genuinely liked the paintings, and we would look at them together and talk about their three-dimensional qualities and the way the vampire appeared to be moving as you walked from one side of the painting to the other. I told John to spot them, and then talk about all the details that Anne and I had observed, as if he had discovered them on his own. He was to become obsessed with them.

I knew Anne would tell him they were not for sale, and John was to become adamant that he would own them both. He was to start bidding on them, and each time, Anne would say something like "I'm so sorry, but I can't sell them." He would go up on his offer to the point of ridiculousness. And you must remember we needed the money very badly. Rent was $3,000 a month, and we had candles and T-shirts and no customers.

It took several whiskey and Cokes to get New York John geared up for the part. While he liked the idea, he didn't want to be the one to act it out. He was shaking a little with anxiety. I finally convinced him to make the walk three doors down and get into the part. I was grinning from ear to ear and couldn't wait to hear what happened. It took much longer than I had anticipated, so I figured John was doing a good job. About twenty-five minutes later, here came John with one of our bags in tow.

"How did it go?" I asked him.

"I couldn't do it," he said in sheer failed embarrassment, guilt all over his face that he had let me down. Then a smile spread as he held up the bag. "But I bought the T-shirt!" Ah, now I had a challenge. John did not realize that he had just made this even better. All those years of being schooled by the goddess of schemers, watching *I Love Lucy*, had equipped me with just the deviousness I needed to pull off this April Fools' caper.

"John! This is perfect! This is better!" I needed to get him back in the mode. He slumped down and looked up at me from the top of his eyes. He had failed and had hoped it was over. I bought him another drink and tried my best to psych him up. My plan was to let John enjoy a couple of drinks, giving the joke time to evolve. When John returned for the second time, it would appear that he had been contemplating the paintings all the while and just couldn't take no for an answer. He would return to offer a ridiculous amount of money for them. An offer Anne could not refuse. I figured she would call me and I would let her go on for a bit before using the April Fools' punch line.

John was nervously taking the last sip of his drink as I said "Okay, champ, it's time. Go in there and act like you just have to have those paintings!" The extra liquid courage had John feeling a little better about his part. I could hardly stand the anticipation, and after about fifteen minutes, the phone rang.

Anne's voice was cheerful yet reserved. Because the customer was right there, she didn't want to seem too anxious, so had to play it cool. In a confident, professional tone, for John's sake, Anne spoke: "We have a customer here who is interested in your two black-and-white paintings".

I stopped her in her tracks. "Anne, come on now, you know those aren't for sale."

"Marita, he is offering $1,500 each." Anne is a good friend and genuinely cared about the success of the shop. She knew it would be hard for me to sell the paintings but also, I'm sure, thought it would be insane for me not to.

"I'm sorry, Anne, I just don't want to part with them at any cost. No." And with that, I hung up the phone.

A few minutes later, the phone rang again. I pictured John, warming to his role.

"Marita, listen." Anne's voice was stern on the other end. Anne already knew my fondness of the day and thought I might not take her seriously. "The customer is now offering $2,500 each, and this is NOT an April Fools' joke," she said, almost in exasperation.

"Well, Anne, it actually is! April Fools!" It took her a moment, and then it hit her. I introduced her to my accomplice. I got her hook, line and sinker. And with that, I created a Johnny White's regular. John came back very pleased with his acting debut. New York John purchased a part-time home in the Quarter and became a regular. My new nickname for him became John the Actor.

10

Whistle While You Work

Not long after I moved to the Quarter and had retired Windex Pete as my guardian angel, I was immediately accosted by, and later, annoyed daily by Perry the Clown, also known as Perry the Hobo. Perry was an obnoxious little guy with a raspy voice, who always carried a rubber chicken. Perry, and his sidekick, whose name I still don't know, worked Bourbon Street, blowing up balloons to look like animals. They also performed/begged on St. Peter Street and often came in for many a beer break at Johnny White's. Their home base however, was often Jackson Square. In fact, Perry could be found there every day. I guess you could say he was a hard worker, because he was consistent and he surely put in some hours. He was often intoxicated and seemed to enjoy his profession. He was dressed much as you would expect a clown to look, only a little dirtier. He had a colorful costume—I'm sure he washed at least once a month, maybe.

Perry would blow up balloons to look like animals, and while he entertained children tourists, his target market was most definitely adults. Perry was a big "B" drinker, meaning he would try to befriend customers in our bar, charm them by making some balloon animals and hope for a free drink in return. We did not look kindly on "B" drinking at our bar, so Perry was pretty good at making it work for him. As long as we felt the customers weren't annoyed, we would leave him be.

My friend Lucinda had moved from 711 Royal because she had met Jimmy, an aspiring film director, not long after I moved into her old apartment. They married, and their son Noah was on the way. It was a fun time for all of us. I was the maid of honor at her wedding in Jackson Square. The reception was at Pirate's Alley Café. After having lived here for just a short three months, I found it so easy to melt into the open arms of the Quarter.

So Lucinda and Jimmy needed more room. They found a dream apartment in the Pontalba Building, overlooking Jackson Square. The first time I saw the apartment, I couldn't get over the view. Truly one of the most beautiful spots I'd ever seen. The view was through a huge oak tree that reached as far as it could, trying to cross the square. Tourists roamed about the square, artists painted and sold their goods against the fence and the tarot card readers, musicians and street performers entertained the crowd.

Street performers—stop! Lucinda rushed to the window. "God damn it!" she shouted. "I'm going to lose my mind! The same whistle all day long. I can't stand it here." I couldn't even begin to entertain the thought of hating it in this gorgeous place. However, Lucinda was referring to Perry the Clown. He had a whistle that had one tone—and one tone only—and it was loud. He would stay in the square and whistle that one tone to draw attention to himself and his balloon animal skills.

I couldn't argue that it was horrifyingly annoying—but the view and the breeze through the trees were simply magical. Yet whistle—whistle—whistle all day long. Lucinda was pregnant after all, so the whistle was most likely ten times more piercingly horrific to her. She closed all the windows and turned up the music, and we pretended to ignore it. Yet that one whistle tone seemed to tap us on the shoulder, trying to grab our attention over and over and over again. Lucinda was quickly making plans to vacate the Pontalba.

It was about a month later that everyone in the Quarter was talking about Perry the Clown. The *Times Picayune* reported that Perry had been arrested for selling cocaine out of his rubber chicken. I suppose that's why he largely targeted adults for his act. For some reason, it wasn't that much of a surprise to me.

We never saw Perry again, so I'm not certain how he ended up in Boston. But a few years back now, Perry made our local news again. He was found dead in his Boston apartment alone. We never learned the cause of death. However, Perry the Clown and his drug-filled rubber chicken will forever be remembered.

11

Mother Superior

My first year at Johnny White's, I was a greenhorn. I was thirty-six years old and just learning what "regulars" meant. In California, I had several bars that I would frequent, but I certainly didn't go to a bar every day, let alone the same bar every day. At Johnny White's, there were a lot of regulars to meet, and I also had a great number of reoccurring regulars, or regular tourists. These are people who lived out of town, but when they came to the Quarter, they spent almost their entire vacation at our bar.

One such group was the Nuns from Wisconsin. Carla, one of my favorites, was the Mother Superior. She reminded me of the actress Margot Kidder. The group of about eight nuns would come down for a long weekend and drink and smoke and play poker, and they would do this once a year. Carla was the ringleader, and she stayed glued to the poker machine almost her entire time here. She had a dry, witty sense of humor and was just fun to be around. The other nuns popped in and out during the weekend, enjoying their freedom.

When they told me they were nuns, I couldn't believe it. But Carla explained it to me that this was their one time a year to get everything out of their systems. While she was pulling my leg, it seemed rational to me, and she was so believable that I went on believing it for several years. J.D. broke the news to me; the nuns were just a women-only group with a good sense of humor. However, they took it seriously. The nuns had several rules, and I only recently learned that it was quite difficult to become initiated into the

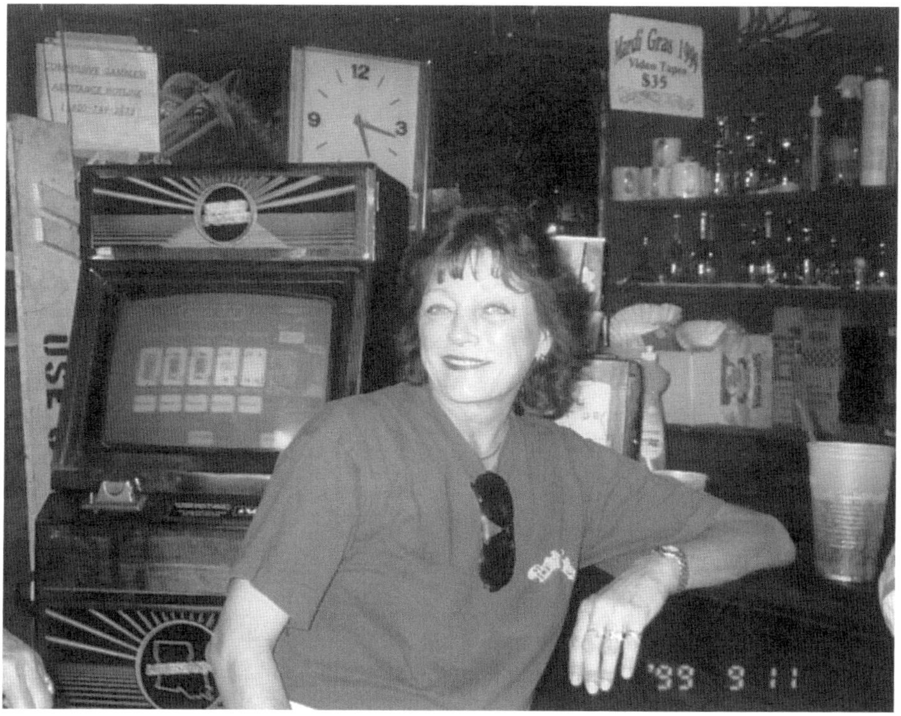

Sister Carla at the poker machine. *Sister Jay.*

group. First rule, no men on the trip, and you cannot hook up on the trip. The other nuns did not want to spend their weekend worrying about one of their members. This was a very strict rule, and if it was broken, you would not be invited to join them again. Theirs was truly a women-only weekend, which prompted them to coin their group "The Nuns."

New members were responsible for securing the hotel and anything else they might need, and that was basically it—simple but strict when it came to the rules. When I eventually discovered that these ladies were not actually nuns, it didn't really matter, because they were nuns to me. Carla has since passed away, and thereafter, Jay became the new Mother Superior, and she takes the job very seriously. In fact, she was extremely upset that someone they had brought along on one of their annual visits for a test run/initiation to nun-hood had come back on her own and posed as a Nun.

This woman came to the sports bar and introduced herself to me as one of the Wisconsin Nuns. Of course, I gave her the usual welcome and didn't have any reason to suspect her to be a poser.

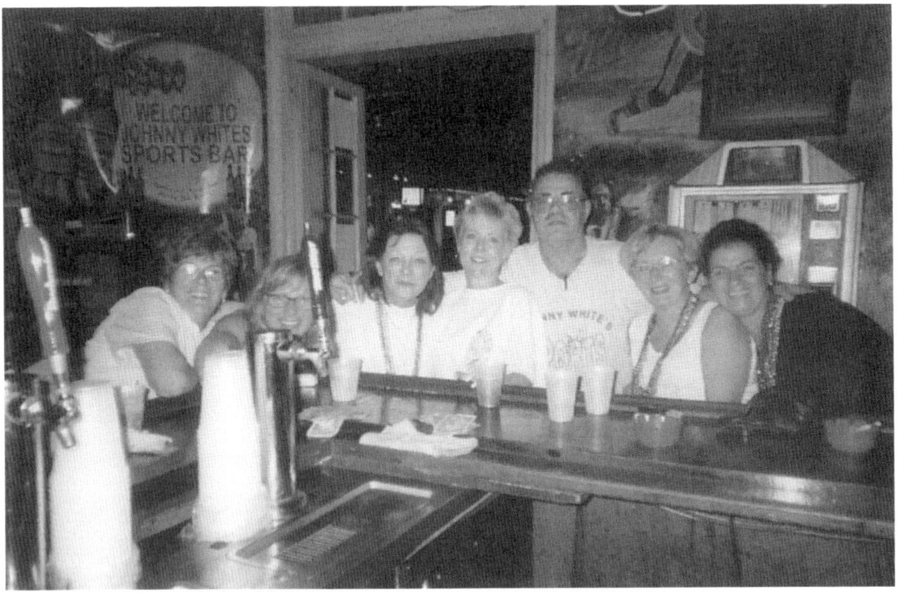

The Nuns, pictured with bar co-owner Tom Hill. *Sister Jay*.

Well, the next time the Nuns came in, I was all excited to tell them I met their other sister a few months prior to that and I had taken good care of her. The Nuns went through the roof. They were all so upset with the poser because they had made it crystal clear to her that she had not met their initiation requirements and that she ruined their short trip. In fact, she was thrown out of the group and was told she would never, not ever, be a Nun.

The ladies explained that she broke the ultimate rule. Not only did she hook up with a tourist of the male persuasion during her short visit here to New Orleans, but she also went missing with him for an entire night and day. That is exactly why the Nuns were so strict with their rules. The poser thought it was all in good fun, but the Nuns worried about her and couldn't relax and enjoy themselves while the poser was missing. This is not why they came to New Orleans. I could see the fury in their eyes as they recollected the experience. I was glad there were no rulers about for fear of being punished just for bringing up the subject.

Jay and I later sat down and had a long discussion about the sanctions of the Wisconsin Nuns while the other ladies weren't around. Then I came up with what I thought was a brilliant idea. I'm very fond of Jay, and I asked her if I could become an honorary New Orleans Nun. She is still thinking it over. She insisted that she had to run it by the other Nuns and see if everyone

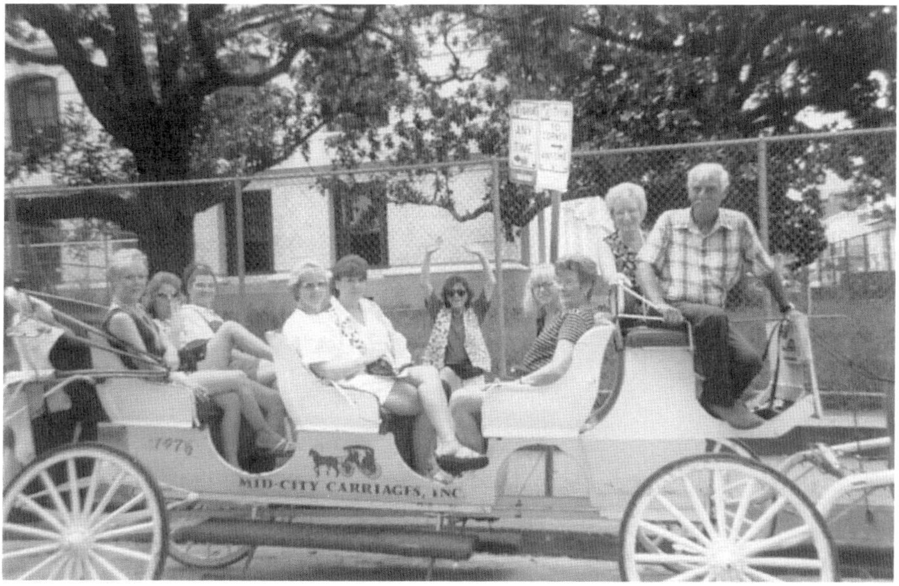

The Nuns taking a carriage ride with J.W.'s regular "Buggy Rick." *Sister Jay.*

agreed to the idea. It would require that I set up their trip to New Orleans whenever they visit, make hotel and restaurant reservations, tours and so forth. I can't really explain why on earth I would add one more thing to my never-ending plate of chores, but the challenge now has me relentless in becoming a member of the Nuns.

12

Be Careful What You Wish For

It was a slow Wednesday night. My shift had just started. I switched the TV in the corner above the poker machine to Animal Planet and started putting randomly scattered liquor bottles in their right places.

Miss Elaine entered the bar carrying a Bud Light in a small brown paper bag so that the top of the can was exposed and easily accessible, a cigarette in the same hand. She waved at me with her free hand and headed right for the poker machine in the back corner by the door to the stairwell.

She wore one of her wigs, and even though it was an obvious embellishment, it looked okay on her. Maybe I was just used to her wigs. Miss Elaine always looked okay. She was about sixty and looked good for her age. Her black skin glowed. Her outfits always matched, and while you could tell she was a thrifty shopper, it was obvious she was thoughtful in putting herself together each day.

She fumbled in her pocket for a bill and slyly motioned for me to come make her some change.

"Now don't you tell him I have this money," she said, looking at the door. "Give me fives."

As I turned to head for the register, she mumbled her usual complaints about her boyfriend, Mr. Robert, and it made me smirk. "He never gives me nothing. God damn man. Thinks I can live on pennies. I have to work every day." And the mumbling continued as I approached with her change. "And give me a Bud Light. He'll pay for it. He'll be here soon."

"Can I get a straw?" I forgot she always drank canned beer and wine splits through a straw.

She put a five in the machine and watched the door for Mr. Robert over her shoulder as she pushed the buttons, now and then mumbling small complaints about her man.

I went back to arranging and tidying up a bit, hoping for a little business later in the evening. But it was summertime.

Miss Elaine's grudge was on my mind—always upset with Mr. Robert and jealous of him to the core.

Mr. Robert, or "Pops" as many people called him, was in his late seventies. He was a small-framed black man who looked his age, but his personality gave him youth. He always seemed happy. Mr. Robert was a street performer. He stood in his colorful suits on a red Coca-Cola crate and sported a large straw hat adorned with a cornucopia of silk and plastic flowers. His gimmick, other than his attire that is, was a toy electric guitar that would play every time a dollar entered his tip jar. He would stand motionless on that crate for hours. He did well though—enough to live off of and buy drinks for Miss Elaine. Much to Elaine's chagrin, he would often buy a round at the sports bar for his friends. Elaine would be steaming mad every time Mr. Robert asked us to put one of the female regulars on his tab. She thought he was fooling around with every girl in the bar. In her mind, the old guy was a regular sex machine. Peeping over her shoulder while Mr. Robert socialized with ladies, her fingers poking harder at the gambling device, jealous rage poured from her every pore.

"Marita, let me have another beer." She called from the poker machine. "Robert will pay for it." I nodded and gave her a second beer and a straw. "He should be here any minute. Probably stopped at Molly's. Thinks I don't know he goes there." You could visually see her taking mental notes of where he should be at this time and getting more upset that he wasn't hurrying to meet her.

She stopped playing poker and sat close to the Bourbon Street entrance. "I'm going to get some money from him tonight though. I'm going to a party this weekend, and I don't have anything to wear. He never gives me any money."

Right on cue, Mr. Robert came through the Bourbon Street door. He was wearing his yellow suit with a red shirt and colorful tie. The bouquet on his head made him even more cheerful than his smiling face advertised.

"Hi dear," he greeted me, smiled in Elaine's direction and put his Coke crate and guitar in the corner on a beer keg, where he always stored it while in J.W.'s. He made his way next to Elaine at the bar. He pecked her on the cheek. "You alright?" he asked, meaning did she need a drink. She ordered another.

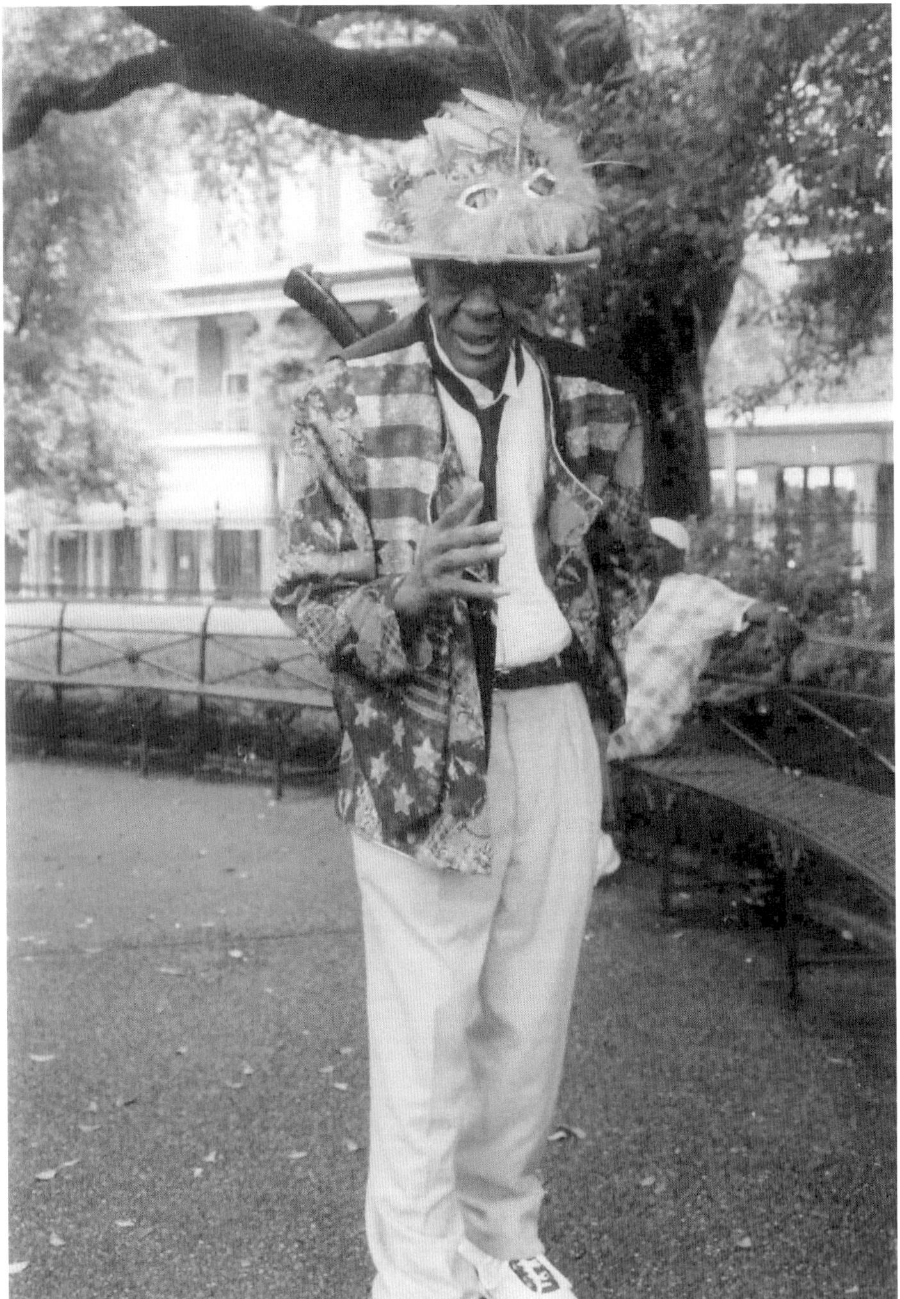

Mr. Robert "Pops" at work. *Byron Penn*.

"How was your night, Mr. Robert?" I asked as I poured him his usual scotch and water.

"Oh wait, just a beer, a draft. Sorry about that dear," he apologized.

"That's what I get for assuming. I'm ready for a cocktail anyway." I put aside the drink and poured Mr. Robert his beer.

I couldn't help but think how opposite they were, Mr. Robert filled with joy and generosity and Miss Elaine filled with disgust and greed.

"How much does he owe you?" Elaine asked me. "Pay her," she said to Robert.

Mr. Robert cheerfully paid the tab.

When I returned with Mr. Robert's change, I finished making my mistake drink and sat down on a stool that a customer, Chris, had brought me from her home so that I could rest my back now and then.

"So," I intruded. "Just how did the two of you meet?" They weren't married; they were just somehow tied to each other. And every night would eventually end for them with an argument and Mr. Robert leaving the bar in a huff, tired of Miss Elaine's aggravation and nagging. It was just part of their routine and now part of the nightly scene at the bar.

"He stole me from another man." Elaine stepped in. "And now he can't take care of me. He should have left me alone."

I looked at Mr. Robert. "Yup," he said. His shoulders jerked up and down, as they always did when he laughed. "Hee hee hee."

"I was just fine." Elaine continued. "I had a good man, a man with money. Gave me everything I wanted. Knew how to treat me. He was in love with me. Lots of men were in love with me back then. He was a good man." She reflected for a moment. "We used to go to a nice bar, not around here. That's where we met Robert."

"Hee hee hee," Mr. Roberts shoulders jerked up and down.

"Well, Robert lied and went and told him that I was sleeping with him, and my man left me."

"What? Is that true Mr. Robert?" I asked with a smile. At this point, I took everything Miss Elaine said with a grain of salt.

"Yup," he owned up to it proudly. "Hee hee hee."

"Well, why'd you do that?" I asked.

"Because I wanted her for myself," Mr. Robert answered, very matter of fact like.

"Mr. Robert! You devil. You didn't!" I was surprised.

"Hee hee hee" Jerk, jerk, jerk.

"Oh yes, he did, and now he can't take care of me. Never gives me any money."

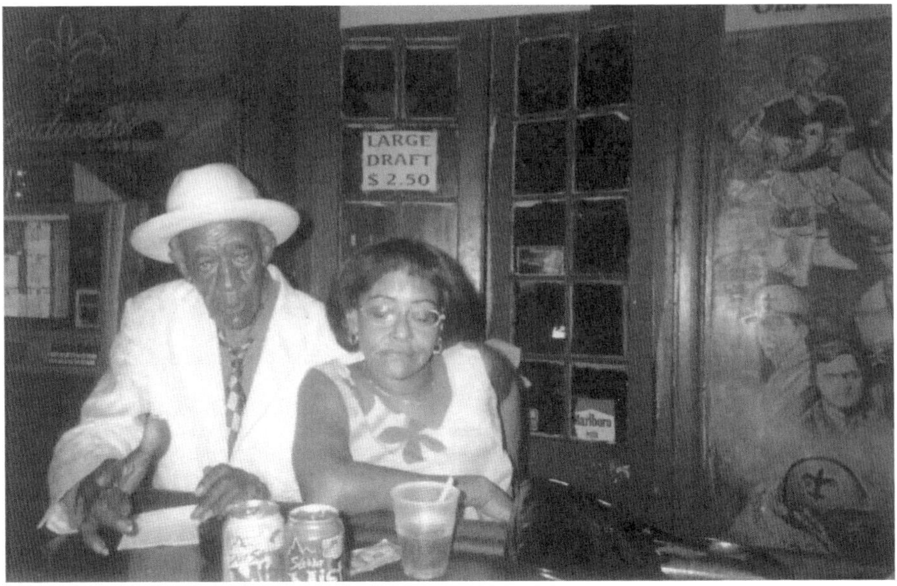

Mr. Robert with Miss Elaine. *Byron Penn.*

Their relationship suddenly made sense to me. Be careful what you wish for. Boy—be careful what you wish for.

It was a special evening for me, getting the scoop firsthand. Mr. Robert's honest joviality was charming, as was Elaine picturing her past and what could have been for her. And now she had created this prison for herself—following the "sex machine on the crate" around, demanding her beer and gambling money on a nightly basis.

However, there really was more to their relationship than met the eye. I'll never forget one evening when Elaine mouthed off to a street hustler who was begging outside the door. The guy had a wasted life at about forty-five years of age, trying to get tips from tourists for giving them directions. Something he said irked Elaine, and she told him off. Well, he came right after her and cursed her out. Mr. Robert came flying off his chair—if that's possible—in her defense. Why, he fought to take his suit coat off so he could show this guy a thing or two. Two of my patrons worked on Mr. Robert, holding him back, while Steve, my boyfriend, went outside and persuaded the guy, pretty much with one look, to get the heck out of there and have more respect for women and his elders.

It took Mr. Robert a few moments to calm down. Elaine felt like a queen, and every one of us in the bar felt warm all over.

Anyway, this evening, Miss Elaine and Mr. Robert seemed to be getting along. Talking about old times and how they met must have brought back some fond memories for the two of them. It had them flirting a little, and on this night, they left without fighting—instead, there was a gleam in Mr. Robert's eyes.

13

A Passion for Horses

Summertime…and the living is easy. Summertime was anything but easy in the French Quarter. Shop owners, bartenders and strippers waited at their posts along empty streets—like an amusement park waiting to open for the fun to begin. The air conditioning at Johnny White's worked at half-mast, when it worked at all, providing us with a sweaty glow while Aaron Neville played on the jukebox.

On one of these days, my neighbor Joe walked by and felt bad for me, sitting there with just one other customer, another Johnny White's bartender I had relieved a couple of hours earlier. It was particularly hot and humid that day. We closed all the doors and hoped that the little bit of air that blew out of the vents would eventually accumulate into some kind of cooling effect, but this was only wishful thinking.

We all desired something extremely cold to quench our thirsts. I suggested a frozen drink from Tropical Isle, the bar across the street. One of its feature drinks is a refreshing concoction that I knew I needed to quench my desire for something cold and wonderful. Joe forgot about his beer and joined the other bartender and me in the invitation of a Tropical Itch. I suppose it was a bit unethical bringing a competitor's drink into our bar, but in the heat of the hot summer moment, I just knew my boss would understand. He might even have joined us in the drink had he shown up.

Even though Joe had been my neighbor for almost a year, we had never had much of a conversation, other than idle chitchat. I did know that Joe went to the racetrack frequently, and as we visited, I was aware that he was keeping some interest in the TV on the wall behind me. A series of races were being shown. "Oh shit!" he said, in the direction of the TV. "Man, I hate when they race fillies against studs. It's so dangerous."

I was disappointed in Joe that he was annoyed by watching a female horse compete against a male. "Just another one of 'those' men," I thought to myself. Joe took a drink of his Tropical Itch and just shook his head.

"It's not what you think," he said. "There was this horse, a filly, Ruffian. She won every race she ever ran. She was amazing. This was about twenty-five years ago. I mean, it wasn't even a contest. This girl had so much heart. She was one in a million."

As Joe started to talk about this horse, he became passionate and animated. This was a side of him I'd never seen before. I realized then that the reason we had never had a conversation before is because he really wasn't particularly interested in anything that was going on around him at the bar. He usually came in, ordered a beer and made small talk before he headed home. He never stayed long, and while he sometimes talked about football, he was pretty even keeled and uninterested. And honestly, I had never been particularly interested in engaging Joe in conversation because his ambivalence actually made him uninteresting to me. However, as I watched him now and listened, his enthusiasm had me completely captivated in a topic I had never found interesting in the past.

I didn't know much at all about horse racing, other than it was cheap to bet on and exciting if you're there. Just after I moved to New Orleans, I was invited to the Fairgrounds by one of Lucinda's friends, Eddie, a burly, fun-loving guy, who at the time tended bar at the Little Tropical Isle. I used to stop in there and visit with Eddie, who would make me the most delicious rum punch. Eddie explained to me that Thanksgiving Day was opening day at the racetrack here, the New Orleans Fairgrounds. The Fairgrounds is only a few miles from the Quarter, and Eddie told me a whole group got together from Johnny White's and went to the races on Thanksgiving. Then they all went their separate ways to enjoy their Thanksgiving feasts. That sounded very appealing to me, so I met everyone at Johnny White's, and we all cabbed it to the track. Someone had already reserved a grand spot for us in the Paddock. We splurged on champagne and oysters on the half shell while we watched the horses prance by and introduce themselves. It was a very civilized way to choose the horse we would eventually bet on. In fact, it was such a great time, that Thanksgiving morning at the racetrack has become a tradition I really cherish. We always met at Johnny Whites' for a Bloody Mary, then headed to the racetrack with our friends.

That's all the horse racing I knew. I picked names I liked and horses that appealed to me. I actually won a couple of races, but I can't say I ever found the subject interesting really—until this day at the bar with Joe. He explained,

> *Ruffian was scheduled to race against Foolish Pleasure, one of the toughest males at the time. So it was the best of the fillies against the best of the males. Everybody was anticipating the race. The hype around it was overwhelming, if you were in the race world. The purse was huge, and side bets were everywhere. It was a big deal, because at the time the war against the sexes was raging as well. Bobby Riggs and Billy Jean King's match had just happened, and this was horse racing's answer to the war of the sexes. In fact, people everywhere were wearing buttons that said "I'm for Ruffian" or "I'm for Foolish Pleasure."*

This event, Joe explained, actually transcended the sport because everyone was interested in the event.

> *When the race started, everyone was on the edge of their seats. There were a lot of those guys, chauvinists I guess, who were saying this race was no contest; Ruffian didn't have a chance. Yet there she was, nose to nose, neck to neck with Foolish Pleasure. Then, as they turned the last bend into the final stretch, Foolish Pleasure started to pull away. Well, everyone went wild, as the commentators were saying things like, "See there, there's no way a filly can beat a male like that." Even as they continued to celebrate Foolish Pleasure's success as he headed toward the finish line, Ruffian didn't stop trying.*

Joe started to choke up, and a couple of tears swelled in his eyes. As he fought to finish his story, the sweat from my brow joined the tears running down my check in a salty mess. "What the commentators and all those people celebrating didn't see," he continued,

> *was that Ruffian continued fighting. Her drive wouldn't let her lose, even though she had run so hard that her ankle broke and her hoof was dangling off her leg. She was running with everything she had on just a stub. Once she crossed the finish line, her jockey and everyone else came to the realization of what had just happened. It was, I think, the most solemn moment in horse racing. Her heart and drive had cost Ruffian her life.*

I was speechless as we sat there in tears. We sipped on our frozen drinks and sat there a moment in total silence. "Wait a minute," I suddenly came to a realization. "Didn't they learn anything from that? I mean they still race fillies against males?"

"Not very often," Joe answered, regaining his composure. Joe looked out the window a moment. "I should tell you about John Henry. You'll like this story." I was truly thrilled that Joe had another story to tell. After all those days of thinking he had nothing to say, I was hanging on his every word.

This is a great story. In fact, this horse is still alive and living a great life in Lexington, Kentucky, at the horse park. Man, John Henry was one of those horses that loved to race. And he won and won and won. He was a real tough horse when he was racing, and he was mean. Kind of the Hannibal Lecter in the horse world. Only certain people were even allowed around him, and he had a special stall that had a steel gate that kept anyone from touching him. It was super reinforced because he would kick and stomp and ruin every stall they put him in. In fact, he got his name because he would tear the steel feed tub off the wall and then stomp on it until it was flat.

Anyway, it was the last race of John Henry's career in the Meadowlands in New Jersey, and he looked really good, as usual. It wasn't his toughest race, but there was a lot of excitement around it because it was his last. It was no surprise when he won.

John Henry was no stranger to going to the winner's circle and getting his picture taken with the roses around his neck, but on this day, his trainer and the jockey couldn't get him to budge. He stood there solid as a rock, stubborn and insistent. Nobody knew what was going on, as they continued attempting to lead him to his celebration. Finally, the jockey saw what John Henry was up to. John Henry was watching the replay of the race on the big screen TV positioned only a short distance away. He watched the screen intently, and not until he watched himself cross the finish line was he ready to accept his praise.

Once again, I was speechless. "I was fortunate enough to go up to Kentucky and meet John Henry in person," Joe said. "It was very intense though. He's still mean as hell to most people, and I had to stand back while my guide gave him Swedish fish candies through the gate."

I gained a real new respect for Joe that afternoon and a new awareness of horse racing. This hot, quiet, otherwise ordinary boring day was made magical by finding a passion in someone who was willing to share.

14

The Perfect Storm

While J.W.'s had the status of the locals' living room, it also was the place to go if there was a tropical storm. J.D. felt that people needed a place to gather if they were planning on staying in the Quarter during a storm. People naturally wanted to see other people once a storm had passed, so while J.D. didn't necessary stay in the city, he made sure the bar was open to act as a refuge point for others. In August 2005, with the threat of Hurricane Katrina coming, many regulars were packing up to evacuate, while several others were making plans to stay put. That night, we left our television on. We woke to a newscaster standing on a roof, reporting that that is exactly where we would be with rats and snakes if we decided to stay.

The feel in the city was eerie—not a soul on the street, warm breezes filling the air, it really was the calm before the storm. My boyfriend and I stopped by Johnny White's to pick up some ice and let everyone know that I wouldn't be back until time for my shift on Thursday. There were several bartenders and regulars who weren't planning on going anywhere, so the bar would be safe. We didn't have locks for the doors, so the bar that never closed would keep its status.

Steve and I ran into two J.W. regulars, Jimmy and Camille, on our way out of town. We bid our goodbyes, innocently expecting to have our lives back to normal in just a few days. Steve's brother, Vernon, lived in Houston, so that's where we were headed. Armed with sandwiches, snacks, sodas and my German Shepherd, Elke, we were on our way to Texas.

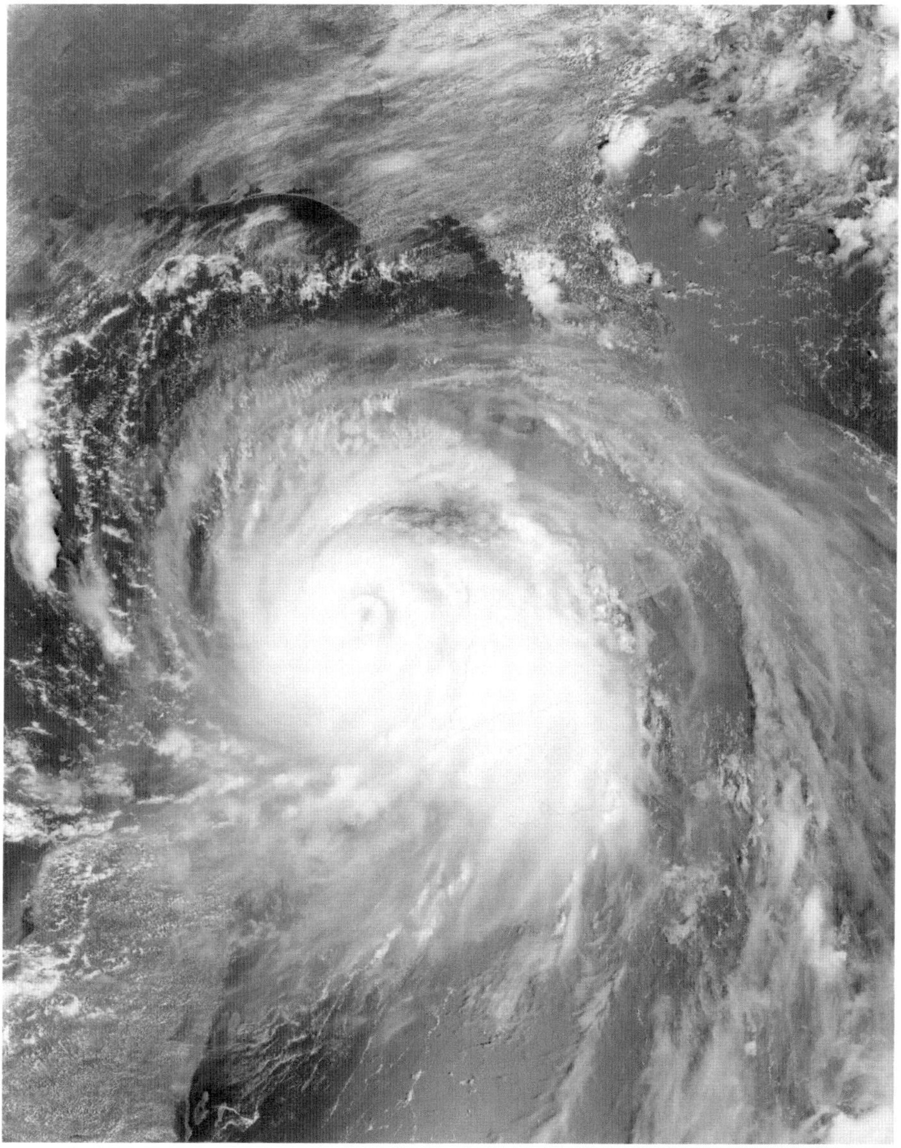

Hurricane Katrina on its way to New Orleans. *Dennis Hallinan/Alamy Stock Photo.*

Normally a five-hour drive, this time it took eighteen. Parts of this trip became terrifying as we were bumper-to-bumper as far as you could see. There were entire stretches where we stayed parked for over a half an hour. People pulled cages with chickens and cats out of their cars to give their pets some fresh air. Now and then strong winds would start, to the point our cars were swaying in the wind. I remember praying that we would get off the road before the storm hit.

Marcie, a J.W.'s bartender; Paul, the janitor; and Bedwyr, a onetime J.W.'s bartender and then regular at the bar, were the three people who kept the bar running during the strange aftermath of the storm. Throughout the storm itself, most of the regulars who stayed behind found refuge in their own homes. During the bands of the storm, Marcie and Paul stayed at the bar and literally had to hold the shutters closed by securing trash bags through loops on the doors and then hold them tightly in place as the winds and rain pummeled down Bourbon Street.

It was our salvation that the phone at Johnny White's never failed to work. The bar had a landline, so electricity wasn't necessary. J.W.'s was the center of our universe, and every time the news media tried to make an already horrific situation more sensational, we would simply call the bar to get the facts.

Nightly news reporters would be stationed outside Johnny White's explaining that the bar had been able to stay open, but now they were being forced to close at gunpoint by authorities while water made its way down

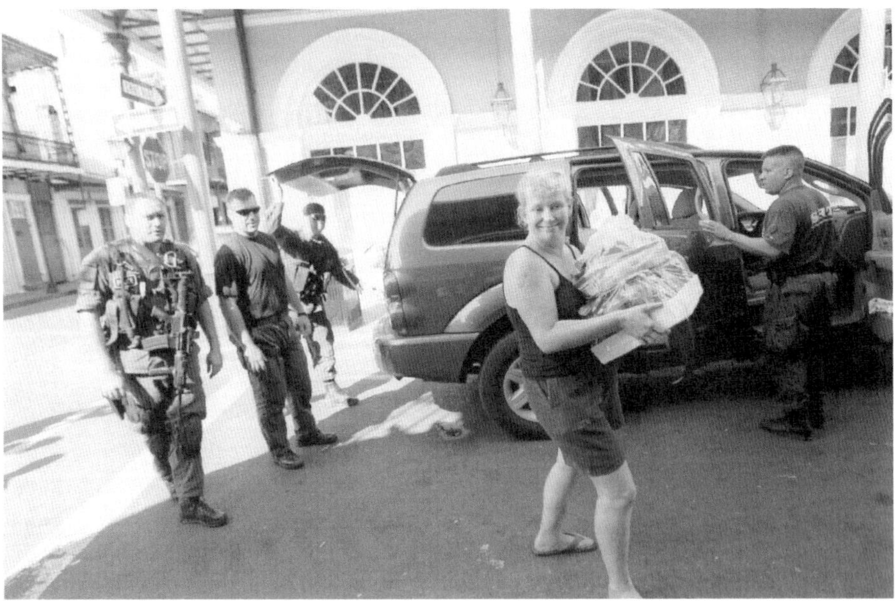

Bartender Marcie accepting supplies from the National Guard. *ZUMA Press Inc./Alamy Stock Photo.*

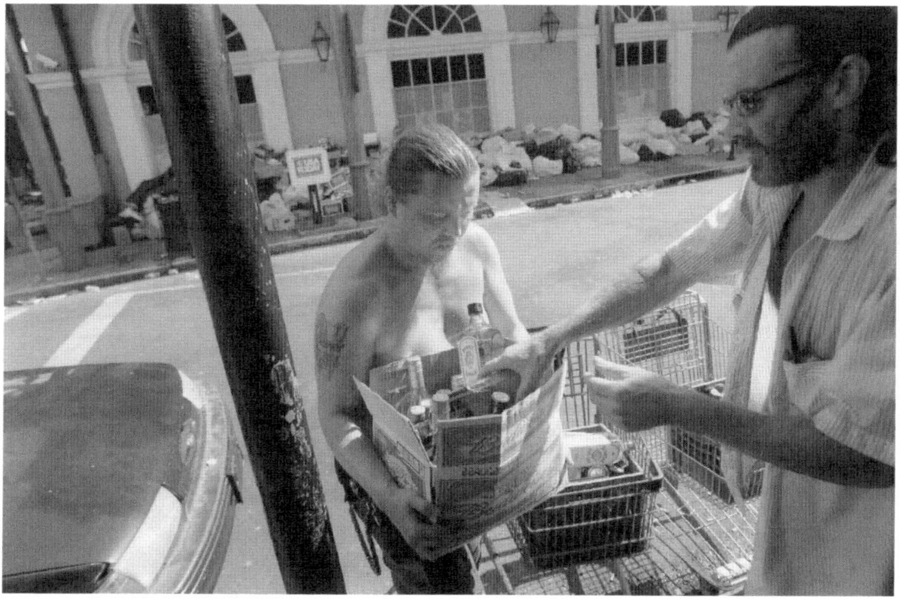

J.W.'s janitor Paul with ex-bartender and bar regular Bedwyr, restocking the bar with supplies from our sister bar MRB. *ZUMA Press Inc./Alamy Stock Photo.*

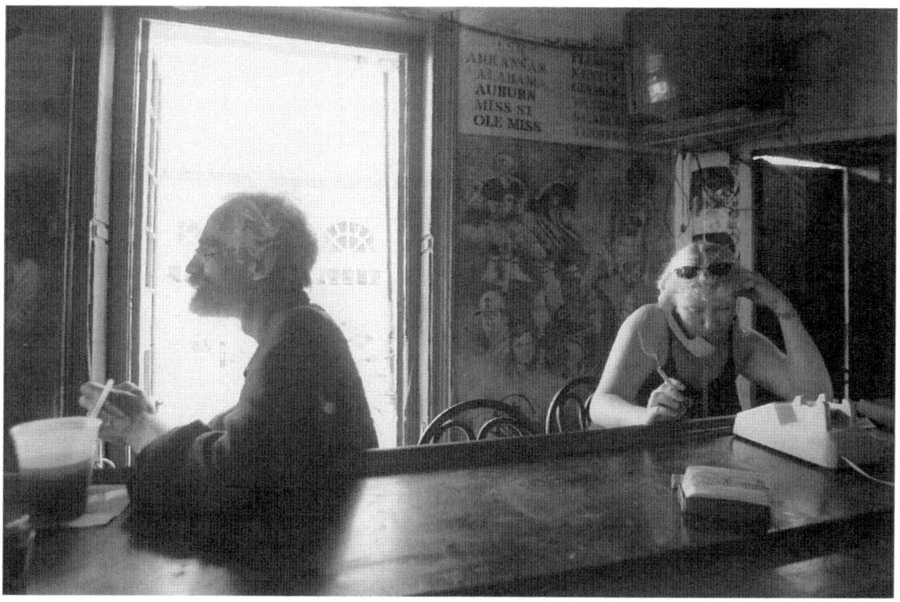

Bartender Marcie manning the phone during the Katrina storm. *Joe Raedle/Getty Images News/Getty Images.*

Bourbon Street. They had managed to film a small section of Burgundy Street, where water had made its way a portion of a block into the Quarter. It was easy to recognize the somewhat flooded street, which was shown repeatedly to add angst to viewers and sensationalize that the Quarter truly might get flooded. Reporters were stretching the truth, in hopes for a better story, at a time when it was extremely important for so many to know what the real situation was. Johnny White's became the only source for the truth. Many regulars who had evacuated would make their daily call to Johnny White's to check in and find out the status of New Orleans.

After about two weeks, a good Samaritan dropped off a generator. Marcie was thrilled to be able to offer coffee to her customers. A CNN reporter entered the bar and, smelling the heavenly scent, said, "Oh, you have coffee!"

Marcie proudly replied, "Yes, we do!"

The reporter then pulled the rug out from under Marcie by asking, "Can you make a Frappuccino?"

Marcie was dumbfounded. She looked at Paul, who was mopping the bar floors, and said, "I don't know—Paul, can you fart in a cup?" The news reporter probably realized at that moment how silly her question had been, but everyone was a little out of touch with reality at this time.

When asked what they remember most about the time just after the storm, I found some interesting recollections from those who held down fort at J.W.'s. Marcie told me it was the paint. Apparently, someone, or perhaps many people, had left paint buckets outside their homes. Katrina had found them and twisted them about the sky and then deposited them on Bourbon Street. Pink, blue and French Quarter green splatterings colored the streets for a very surreal antidote to the gray sadness the storm brought with it.

Several others immediately spoke of the aggressive mosquitos that had most of those "camping" in the Quarter pocked so fiercely they appeared to be going through puberty. As I interviewed the select few who stayed behind and battened down the hatches, keeping the bar running so that the city's denizens would feel safe and connected to civilization, I was touched by the camaraderie they experienced. They took it upon themselves to volunteer for specific jobs, such as gathering food, cooking, caring for animals left behind, manning the phone and eventually finding ice. Survival mode set in, but the fact that the headquarters was in fact a bar made the experience a bit more enjoyable. A place where people generally go to socialize would put a spin on the experience, making it seem more normal than it would have if everyone were forced into a random facility.

WE WERE STILL HOPEFUL that we would be heading home soon, but while the French Quarter was basically safe, it was no small feat getting back to New Orleans. It ultimately took us a month and a half to make it back to a still desolate Quarter. Being among some of the first who made it back, there was still a curfew nightly at 6:00 p.m., no business and the strange sensation of countless refrigerators standing on the sidewalks of every street, creating an aroma through the city so pungent I can still smell it when I recount those days. But we had Johnny White's. No sooner did we drop our belongings at our apartment than we made our way down to the bar to see our friends and catch up on their experiences.

Those who stayed behind had experienced a unique "adventure" in the safety of Johnny White's, from ready-to-eat meals finally arriving through the National Guard and soldiers surveilling and protecting the Quarter's empty streets. The Eighty-Second Airborne also checked on the bar, bringing food,

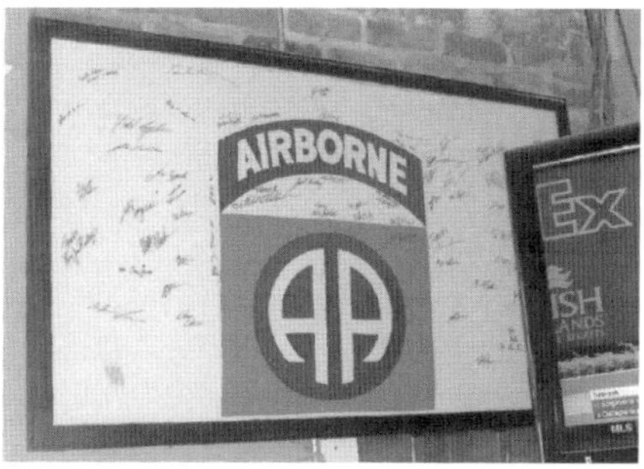

Left: Eighty-Second Airborne flag, signed by soldiers as a token of their support for J.W.'s staying open during the storm. *Author's collection.*

Below: National Guard patrolling streets around Johnny White's. *ZUMA Press Inc./ Alamy Stock Photo.*

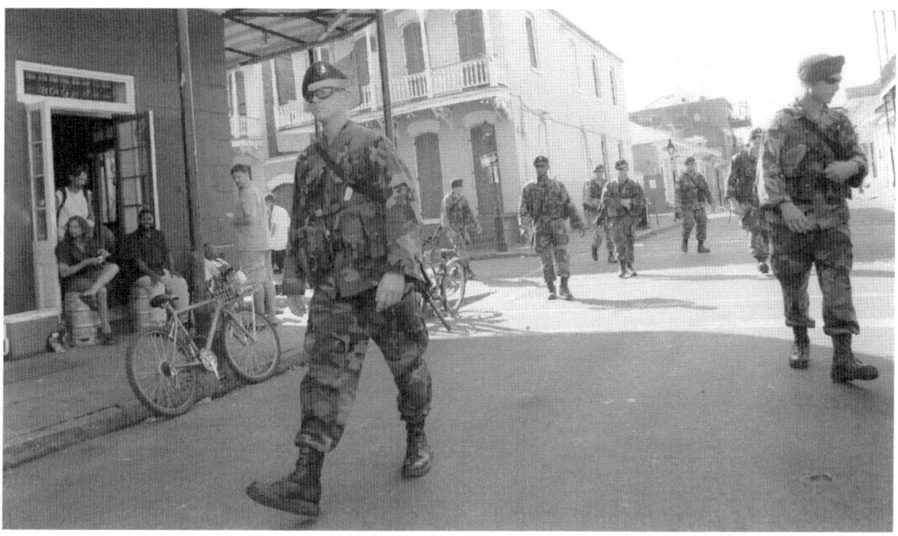

water and other supplies. As a token of their support for the bar staying open, they brought Marcie at the bar a flag with all their signatures—it was later hung from the ceiling.

J.W.'s regulars devised plans to avoid the 6:00 p.m. curfew by ducking between cars on their way back to the bar. Often, to avoid confrontation, when the authorities would make their rounds at curfew time, the regulars would grab a quick drink and sit staggered on the stairwell, hiding behind the door to the bathrooms until the coast was clear.

15

No Good Deed Goes Unpunished

After being gone for so long after Katrina, it was a very strange time, and I found myself having long talks with locals regarding their individual experiences over a drink, or a mistake, while I was tending bar. I wanted to catch up and hear all that I had missed. One of our regulars, local artist Jimmy La Lande, known in the Quarter only as Lala, had one of the most colorful stories I have ever heard.

Jimmy was an unusual guy. He was mostly cheerful, he flirted a lot and he drank too much. He did have some talent though. Jimmy, who had once painted with Andy Warhol, had a unique medium. Jimmy painted on clear plastic. People in the bar joked that he painted on shower curtains, but I own a couple of his pieces, and his craft is quite difficult, in that he paints the foreground first and the background last. Jimmy did large pieces for festivals and often traveled to New York and foreign countries for his art unveilings.

I remember walking up to the bar one day and watching two of our bartenders straighten Jimmy up on his bicycle. They each took a side, walking along with him and then speeding up before finally letting him go. He was too drunk to get started on his own but assured the guys that if they got him started, he could keep going. So there was that.

Jimmy recollected for me an experience he had just one week after Katrina. Having made Johnny White's home base, the folks who stayed behind found it necessary to divvy up daily duties. There was someone on phone duty, someone in search of ice, a few people to provide food, a few people to watch over the bar and, of course, several folks to serve liquor.

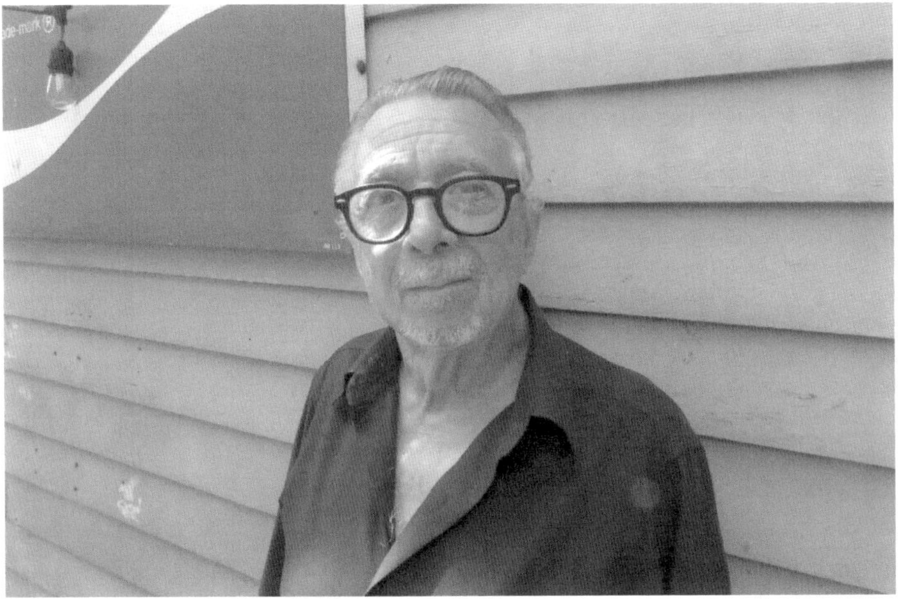

Artist Jimmy La Lande. *Author's collection.*

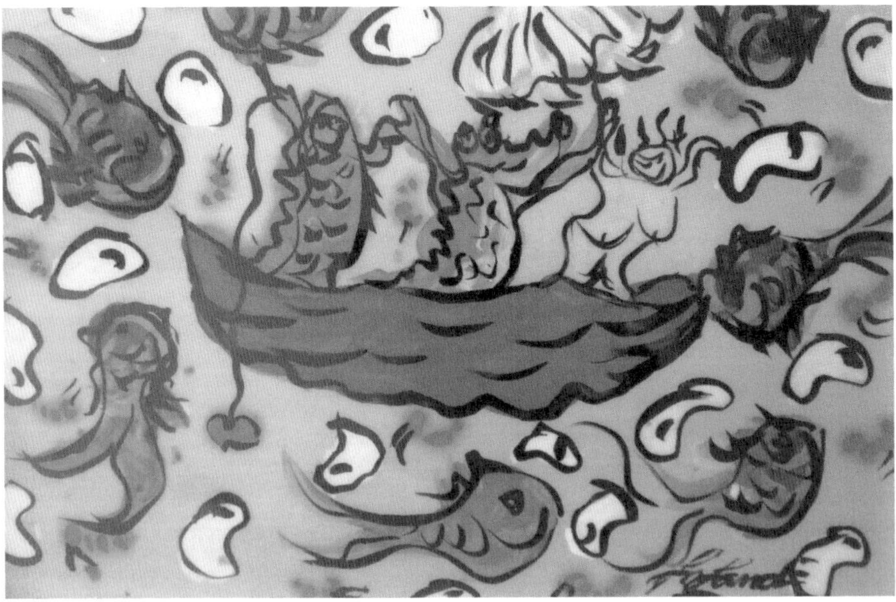

Artwork by artist Jimmy La Lande. *Author's collection.*

Jimmy took over providing for the animals that were left behind in the French Quarter and in the Bywater, a neighborhood just outside of the French Quarter. Many evacuees thought they would be back in three or four days. They filled up cat bowls with loads of food and water, never thinking they wouldn't be able to return for some time. Even dogs were found locked up in temporary situations. Jimmy went to the homes of people who called the bar and asked for assistance with their pets. When he was finished with that, he would go door-to-door to see if any pets were in homes that had been temporarily vacated. He would then break in through a door or window and, after caring for the pets, would leave his business card, alerting the home owner of his visit there.

The National Guard and other organizations dropped off food at the bar. Jimmy would load the bags of food on his bicycle and head off for duty. On one such day, Jimmy was heading through the Bayou St. John neighborhood with two big bags of food draped over his bicycle basket. He was sporting a backpack filled with cans of food and various supplies for himself. Dripping sweat from the overwhelming heat and humidity, he was looking forward to completing his visit and heading home. That's when he happened upon a group of young black neighborhood children. First, not thinking much of it, he greeted them and anticipated peddling by. However, they started for Jimmy and told him that they wanted his bike. While still peddling, he said that would be impossible, as he was on a mission to feed animals. Well, the kids were relentless and started to shout at Jimmy that they had guns. Jimmy started to pedal faster and faster. Then he heard three quick gunshots. It was a small gun, like a .22, he thought. Jimmy said he heard the gun—pop, pop, pop—and it inspired him to peddle faster yet.

He felt something running down his leg—this couldn't be happening, he thought. Jimmy was afraid to look, but he caught a glimpse of red liquid oozing down his jeans. A series of thoughts came to Jimmy. Now what? Someone would have to go out of their way to take care of him now, and they would have to take him somewhere, but where? He didn't want to be a burden; he wanted to help. Who would feed the animals?

Jimmy peddled until he felt he was out of range of the children and somewhere safe. He got a good look at the crimson liquid, thick and red, soaking his jeans. Yet he felt no pain. Perhaps his adrenaline was keeping him from feeling anything. He touched the liquid, and it was cold and felt strange. He raised wet fingers to his nose, and the substance had an unusual odor, reminiscent of—no, could it be? He tasted it. Sure enough, it was tomato sauce. Jimmy took off his backpack and pulled out a can of Chef

Boyardee, dripping liquid out of two holes: the bullet's point of entry and its point of exit.

Still shaking, Jimmy laughed out loud with relief. He never would have believed a can of Chef Boyardee could save the day.

There is a tremendous problem with a segment of the youth in New Orleans. But the problems stem from their parents and their parents before them—that is, if they have parents at all. Many of our city's children have no role models to look to, no discipline or guidance, and it has led to a huge problem that would take chapter upon chapter to discuss.

Luckily, the event did not deter Jimmy from making future trips to help animals. He just chose safer routes.

16

A Clutter of Rodents

It was a humid New Orleans morning, and I was running late for my shift at the bar. A loose stone on the sidewalk shifted under my foot and splashed a mixture of water and leftover beer over my toes and into my sandals. The mixture of leftover liquids that filled the street crevices is known as French Quarter Stew. Well, this stew seeped in-between my toes and down to the safety of my arch where it found refuge, and each step I took was a constant reminder of its presence there. Today, I really wasn't in the mood for it.

Since the storm, I had inherited the morning shift at the sports bar Monday through Friday and one afternoon shift on Saturdays. After two and a half years of working graveyards, I thought anything else would be a breeze. Alas, to my surprise, the morning shift was ultra-unusual. I had to brace myself each day for what I would walk into.

It was a combination of locals, tourists and bartenders who had finished their shifts in the early morning hours and were either heartily celebrating or just having a couple of drinks to unwind. Many times regulars would bring tourists with them, to show off the bar—kind of like an adult version of show and tell. Often there were unruly tourists who were thrilled to have found "the bar that never closed" to continue their state of drunken stupor. Some of them I think felt that being at the sports bar was a lesson in history. They actually felt they were getting some New Orleans culture while drinking themselves silly. "As seen on CNN," one drunkard would slap his partner on the back. "When do you guys close?" he would ask, just to hear the bartender holding court say…"We never close." It was oh so charming.

Just after Katrina, we saw an influx of workers at the bar, either celebrating their weekly paychecks or just arriving for a coffee to start their day. We were the post-Katrina French Quarter's answer to Starbucks.

It was an unusual time. Our usual questionable customers who went by nicknames like Smiley and Book of Knowledge were suddenly replaced by a whole other level of characters with nicknames like Squirrel, Mouse, Skunk and Weasel. It was indeed a clutter of rodents.

Not having been here through the storm or the immediate aftermath, it seemed only fitting I be tolerant of the situation and feel things out before putting some guidelines back in the bar. After all, I was gone for a month and a half and really had no idea what it was like in the Quarter during that time. All I had were the horror and hilarious stories shared by my fellow bartenders. I knew it would take a little time for everyone to come back to reality. So I sat back and watched as those around me started to level off.

I remember spending one morning serenaded by two Hispanic workers. One had a guitar with five strings that had been placed on the top shelf of a liquor cabinet, almost as some trophy or memorabilia from the storm. The other fellow was howling cheerfully to the Spanish ditty the guitar player was attempting to strum. They were amiable fellows, but unfortunately, the more they drank, the more familiar they felt they could become with me. I suppose they were harmless enough, but I kept my guard up. I ended up having them teach me the words in Spanish that would allow me to throw them out in their native tongue. "La puerta está ahí!" They chanted and laughed all the way out the door.

It was a strange time alright, but I decided embracing it was the best choice. Working through the changes and idiosyncrasies of the hurricane aftermath was an experience that ultimately, I think, made our city stronger. It bonded those of us who had already been engaged in a relationship with New Orleans to her even more.

For those of us who know what it means to miss New Orleans, New Orleans is like part of our family. It's the breast from where we drink to get our nourishment, the energy for our souls. She is the mother who embraces us, the mother we want to protect, and the brother whose shortcomings we tolerate one day and who we are proud of the next. She has made us proud, she has made us sad, she has let us down, she has made us feel euphoric, she is family!

LURKING IN THE SHADOWS

On one of these mornings, I braced myself while approaching the bar, anticipating the worst. I could hear the jukebox more than a block away. Then I could see it was crowded as I made the block. Tourists were dancing, singing, laughing. My heart shrank ten sizes as the Grinch took over my entire psyche.

Freddy, a regular who played the keyboard at a local club for a variety show, played air piano on the bar, reveling in the fun. I wanted to smack him right in the stomach as I walked past him to my post.

"Hey babe, wanna dance?" Someone shouted in my direction. I ignored them as I greeted Marcie, the graveyard bartender, and grabbed my bank. I looked around briefly—Marcie was enjoying herself almost as much as her clientele. Freddy was in the middle of the crescendo, and some girl was singing "Redneck Woman" at the top of her lungs. I wanted to disappear. It was 7:10 a.m.

Marcie introduced me to Sissy from Mississippi. She quickly snapped a picture of Marcie and me on her disposable camera. Apparently, she had been left in New Orleans by her boyfriend, who had been accompanying her on a road trip. She was left in the Quarter with nothing but a bag of clothes and a few dollars. She was a dim-sel in distress. Things couldn't have been dimmer really. Yet here was Sissy, making the very best of her situation. I believe it was the highlight of her trip.

Sissy was young, cute and full of enthusiasm. The fact that she had been abandoned in New Orleans didn't seem to faze her. In fact, she was ultra-keen to the fact that she had secured a stripping position at a club on Bourbon. She just needed to make enough money to get a bus ticket back home to her three-year-old daughter. This was her forced escape, and I believed she would milk it as long as she could.

Sissy spent oodles of time on her cellphone reassuring her mother that she was doing just great and would be home in no time at all. Meanwhile, she danced and must have sung "Redneck Woman" ten times a day while reiterating whenever possible how much she loved our bar and how much she loved Marcie.

Sissy had befriended a French Quarter character known as "Shadow," a middle-aged black man who was always impeccably dressed. He had a style about him and always decorated himself with a large gold chain from which hung an even larger golden cross.

Shadow made no secret about the fact that he had spent several years in Angola, a maximum-security prison. For what he was imprisoned, I don't recall, and I'm not certain I ever knew. In prison, Shadow had honed his artistic craft. In fact, a few of his illustrations had been published in some sort of a coffee table art book. He proudly carried this book with him, along with a variety of sketches he hoped to sell bar to bar. We were on his daily route.

We must have been the last stop, actually, because more often than not, Shadow was asleep at the bar on my arrival. Peacefully slumped in the corner as the bar happened around him, he was in his comfort zone.

Anyhow, Sissy was fond of Shadow as a newfound friend in New Orleans, someone who had taken her under his wing. She was truly interested in his stories and enjoyed his attention and admiration. Sissy was nice to everyone and very much enjoyed flirting and leading every lonely French Quarter male to believe she was just one more drink away.

Sissy would dance around Shadow, laughing, and I think sincerely enjoying herself. It wasn't long before they were almost inseparable. I recall that morning after morning they would get some drinks and sit on the stoop across the street talking and laughing for hours. Many times, others would join them, but it was always Shadow right there lurking nearby, and more often than not, he'd be right in the scene.

Night after night, morning shift after morning shift, Sissy entertained Shadow after her shifts at the strip club. This middle-aged man actually became a shadow to this misplaced, stripping ingénue. It became more repulsive to me daily. The situation really gave me a shudder every morning that I came upon them at the bar. Sissy was innocently flirting with Shadow, and I felt he was taking it as something more. It was such a strange relationship—Sissy, knowing exactly where she was, and Shadow having no idea where he stood. Yet he acted confident, like he knew his place was to watch over her.

On one enlightening morning, Sissy was absent from the scene. Shadow was engaged in a conversation with another male at the bar. It was a quiet morning, so I was cleaning and listening to the morning news while Shadow and his friend conversed.

Then I overheard Shadow telling his companion all about Sissy. How she dances around him sexually—how she's so friendly and fun. I thought to myself that this grown man over fifty can't honestly be this delusional. To me, the entire situation seemed so transparent. Sure, Sissy was flirtatious and definitely overstepped the boundaries of leading Shadow on. But it was so obvious after all these mornings that she had no intention of taking her situation with Shadow any further than its current disgusting faux courting stage.

I'd finally snapped and laid into Shadow. "Shadow! Give me a break. Isn't it obvious to you that Sissy doesn't have a romantic interest in you in the least? I mean you should be ashamed of yourself—even considering the thought. I mean really Shadow. Here you sit sulking over her like there was really a chance. Why don't you leave that little girl alone and stop hovering around her like a puppy dog!"

Shadow just shook his head at me. "You don't get it all," he said. "You're on a whole other wavelength. You see, like I was telling my friend here, the girl is all over me. I mean—really all over me—dancing suggestively and carrying on, and all the while, always insisting on taking those damn photos of us together with her cheap-ass cameras, those throwaway kind."

I nodded in understanding, because everything he had said to this point was true.

"You know my record. My prison background—my time in Angola. I want to stay clean, and I am. But you know as well as I do, by the way that girl is behaving, all over town, out all night, without a care in the world. I

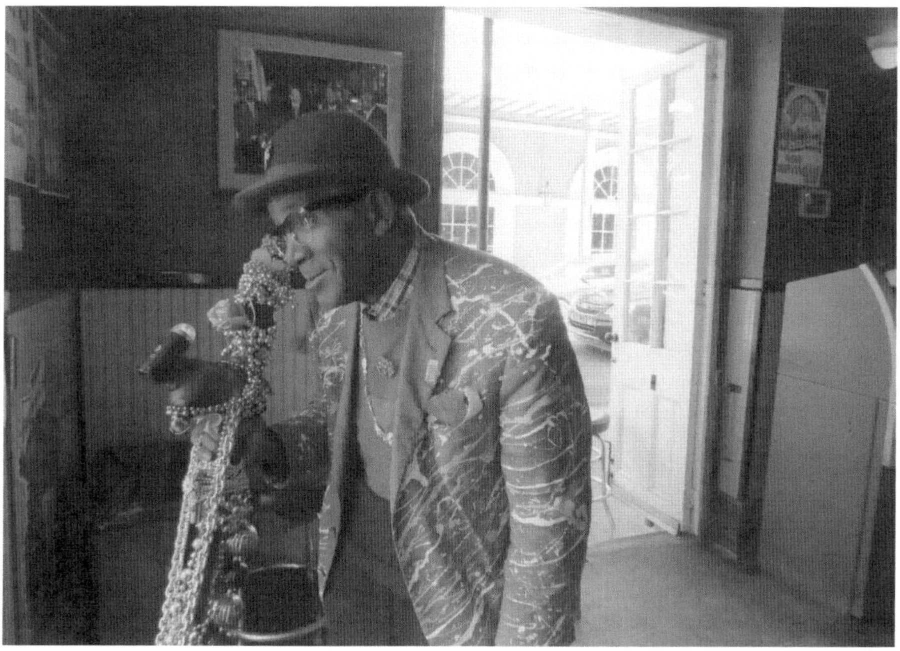

Regular "Shadow" at Johnny White's. *Author's collection.*

mean she's wild that one. Something bad is going to happen to her. But the first day I met her she's all over me with that damn camera. Now, who do you think they're gonna come looking for when that bad thing happens. When she ends up in the river or some damn where, cause of her careless behavior. They're gonna find those cameras, and then they're gonna find me.

"So I'm stuck like chuck. I'm getting in deeper and deeper, more and more photos because I can't let nothing happen to her. Yeah, I'm hovering all right. I'm her Goddamn Shadow. I'm her Goddamn bodyguard. I have to protect her, to protect my ass."

"I mean I like her okay and all, but I wish I'd never met her. It's damn stressful and draining following her from bar to bar, staying up all night, every night. I can't wait 'til she goes back home to Mississippi. It'll be like a Goddamn vacation to me."

It hit me like a frying pan over the forehead. I hadn't expected this at all. It was very enlightening. Shadow was forced to be Sissy's shadow. Talk about poetic justice.

17
Respect

After Katrina, I no longer worked nights. While pre-storm I had enjoyed working the graveyard shift, I'd gotten my fill of nighttime bartending and it was just no longer my thing. I'd stick with my morning sitcom crowd and enjoy the entertaining mix of locals and tourists during the day.

That being said, one evening in the fall of 2011, I got a call at my shop from the swing shift bartender. She said she was sick and couldn't find anyone to fill her spot. The shift was only 6:00 p.m. to midnight. I mustered up my enthusiasm for being a team player, ignored my recent dislike for after dark drink mixing and made my way to the bar. I had come to enjoy my morning shift with day drinkers and really didn't want to get back into serving those who came out at night.

I entered Johnny Whites and found it empty except for Stephanie, the bartender, and the back of Beckhouse, a regular who was slumped over the bar. Beckhouse worked as a doorman at various nightclubs. I'm not sure of his real name, but he got the nickname Beckhouse from an old girlfriend. The name seemed cartoonish to me and very much suited his cartoon-like persona. He stood about six-foot-four and was stocky and out of shape, but not fat. Beckhouse was a young soul and actually reminded us of a big baby. While Beckhouse was pretty goofy, he was also caring and kind and would do anything for his friends. He was the sort of guy you found yourself wanting to look out for.

Well, when I walked in and Beckhouse caught a glimpse of me taking my place behind the bar, a look of terror came upon his face. "You're working?" he asked reluctantly. While I ordinarily didn't particularly care for Beckhouse's patronage, it was puzzling to me why he was so horrified to see me. Honestly, I felt a little put off by his comment.

I turned on the charm when responding, and he composed himself. When I asked him what the problem was, he explained that Sandy, the bartender I was covering for, had a deal with him. She would allow Beckhouse to keep his street clothes behind the bar while he went out on Bourbon Street in his costume to make tips. I didn't know that Beckhouse had a side gig. He would then frequently pop in and buy a quick shot, tip Sandy well, and then head back out to Bourbon. He desperately tried to appeal to my business sense, emphasizing that it was a good money-making endeavor for us both. Sweet.

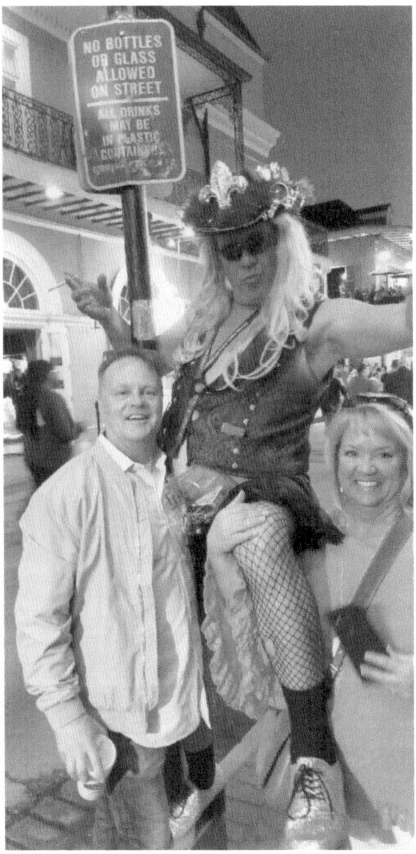

Beckhouse at work, pictured with tourists Lisa Payne and Randy Jackson of Atlanta, Georgia. *Author's collection.*

I was scared to ask what the costume consisted of because I suspected it may have involved a pink tutu Beckhouse had found in the bar the previous Mardi Gras. Used and tossed about the jukebox, it was about to be thrown out with the morning trash. Beckhouse, however, rescued the item. With a gleam in his eye, he decided to model the piece for his contemporaries at the bar. The gesture proved to be great comic relief, and Beckhouse was the center of attention, getting cheers, laughs and encouragement from the crowd. Therewith, an epiphany swallowed Beckhouse. The beginning of a beautiful financial endeavor was created.

I considered the offer. I wasn't sure if our 6:00 p.m.–to–midnight crowd would want to tolerate a clown while enjoying a cocktail. It was a pretty unsettling sight, Beckhouse in his costume, the little there was of it. I was afraid it would be too intimidating and result in customers leaving the bar. I deliberated briefly and came up with what I thought was a reasonable solution. I would allow Beckhouse to engage in his street performing and use the bar as a pit stop. However, we would have a code word between us. If I felt the bar would be uncomfortable with his presence, I would use the code word and Beckhouse would collect his street clothes and vacate the premises for the evening. It seemed reasonable, and he agreed. I wanted to simply use the word *enough*, but Beckhouse whined that it wasn't interesting enough and pleaded with me to use *code red*. Beckhouse disappeared into the bathroom to change into his costume. I had half-forgotten he was in there because it took some time. Then he made his entrance. Since he found that pink tutu, he had elaborated on his costume to a degree that was beyond ridiculous. He had acquired another tutu: black, sheer, with white trim. He sported an elaborate bra, and I cannot even begin to speculate as to how he acquired it. Black fishnet stockings led to sparkling black high heels, and the whole ensemble was topped off with a straight black wig and cowboy hat. I was speechless.

It was a pretty slow night, and Beckhouse had popped in several times over the past few hours, ordering his Oil Slick shot (Rumple Minze with a splash of Jägermeister). He would open his bra, decorated with sequins and gems, count the money that fell from the two cups, pay, tip me and leave as he had promised.

I hadn't heard of an Oil Slick before. I was used to Dead Nazis, which is half Jäger and half Rumple. An Oil Slick was mostly Rumple with just enough Jäger to slip-slide through the clear liquid, giving the illusion of oil in water. I had made the first one wrong, with extremely too much Jäger. So, I set it aside. Now that I was settled in and waiting for business, I took the shot and contemplated Beckhouse.

Shortly thereafter, Steve closed our shop and joined me at Johnny White's. We got to talking about vampire business, and I forgot all about Beckhouse. Steve had met and seen Beckhouse on several occasions at the bar in his street clothes. But if I had thought about it, I would have forewarned Steve of Beckhouse's choice of street performer wear. It was so ultra-ridiculous that is was truly shocking to watch Beckhouse walk into a room.

Anyhow, Steve and I were enjoying a cocktail, and here came Beckhouse all in a huff. I would have paid to watch Steve's expression at Beckhouse's entrance. However, what we were about to experience next was priceless. Beckhouse stood in the door stomping his feet, momentarily speechless. We watched in anticipation as he gathered his composure and found the words to articulate his disgust. "It's terrible out there!" he snorted.

"What no tips, hon?" I asked, not surprised.

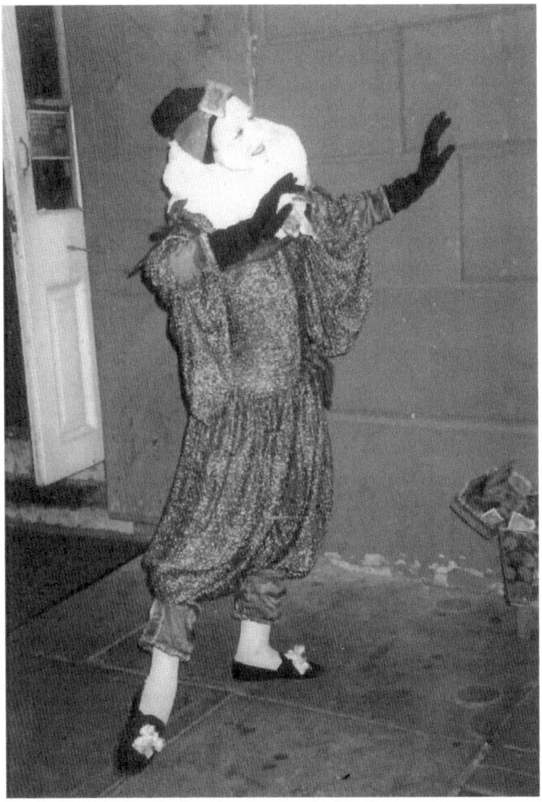

Left: Street performer Suzanne stationed outside of Johnny White's. *Byron Penn.*

Below: Street performers Uncle Louie and Mr. Robert "Pop" taking a break with a regular at J.W.'s. *Byron Penn.*

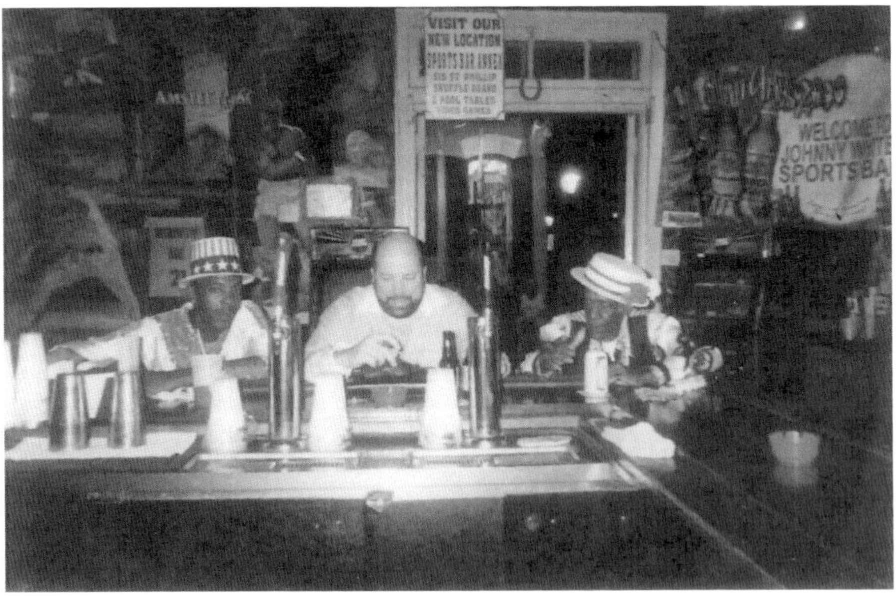

"No, the tips are great," he said as he opened his bra and wads of bills rolled onto the bar. Steve and I sat there puzzled, waiting for Beckhouse to explain. "They're just all over me. Pinching my ass and grabbing my titties," he complained. "These guys were groping me all over. They think that just because they give me money and because I'm in costume, they can touch me however they want." He paused for a moment.

"I just want to be respected," he said, standing center stage in a tutu, bra, fishnets and heels.

There were street performers on Bourbon Street who could absolutely demand respect. Some were true professionals, like Suzanne the mime, with her elaborate costumes. She had professional dance training and looked just spectacular dancing when given a tip. Or Uncle Louie, who wore an Uncle Sam getup and stood motionless while holding a leash with a stuffed dog he had named Willy at the opposite end. These performers had a craft of sorts and were professionals.

Beckhouse stood in his monstrosity of an outfit molesting a Bourbon Street pole. That was his shtick, yet all he asked for was a little respect.

18
Never Hurt a Bunny's Feelings

It was a quiet New Orleans summer morning. As I walked into the sports bar, I was immediately approached by J.W. bartender Jen P. wearing a Playboy Bunny getup. Little did I know this would be the day Jen and I became friends.

J.D. was known for hiring bimbos whenever possible, and initially, this is how I'd summed up Jen. She used to be a dancer, and the minute I met her, I just knew she wouldn't last long at J.W.'s. Our regulars could be a tough crowd, and if they didn't like you, they would make sure J.D. knew it.

I had already had to have a talk with her about her attire at the request of several of our regular customers who found it impossible not to stare at her nipples while they were sipping their drinks. Both of her nipples were pierced, and she made sure everyone knew it by sporting thin, see-through clothing. She was particularly disliked by the female portion of our customers, but even the men had mentioned feeling somewhat uncomfortable regarding her sense of pride in her piercing. Their nickname for her was "chest of drawers," as her nipple rings were just about the size of a handle you might pull on to slide open a drawer. I recall Jen being appalled at my request for her to dress more appropriately. I explained that even though we were a Bourbon Street bar, we were really more of a "family establishment," meaning husbands and wives went there together, and that our regulars found it a bit tasteless. She laughed and made a slight effort to heed my request.

I'm sure Jen lacked fondness for me, as I did for her. I was just counting the days when she would become another past Johnny White's Bar bimbo.

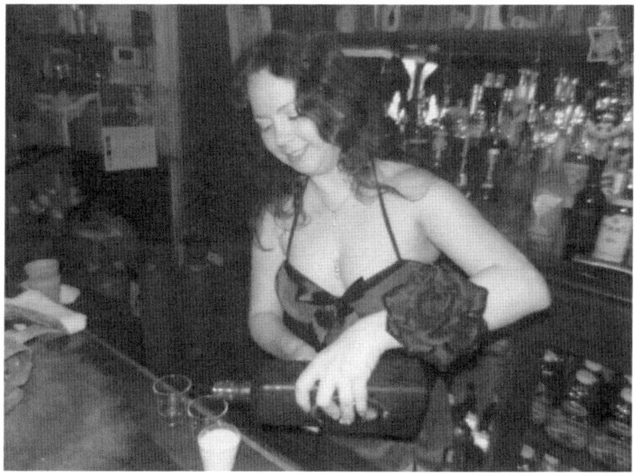

Bartender Jennifer, without the bunny ears. *Zach A. Lbarran.*

Anyhow, on this particular day, Jen had something important to say. There were only two customers at the bar: our regular Angel, who'd had permanent fangs implanted in her mouth to accentuate her look for her vampire and ghost tour business, and a fellow she had brought into the bar with her. Jen led me to our bathroom behind the bar. She was physically upset. Her bunny ears shook with every angry motion of her head as she expressed her concerns.

"That motherfucker with Angel took my tip money," she told me. She explained that he had been very eager to do something for her all night long. He offered to take out the trash, to adjust her ears, and to get her ice. She finally allowed him to get her ice, just to get him off her back. However, instead of just setting the buckets on the bar as other customers do when they help us, he came behind the bar and set the buckets down right next to where the register and her tip cup sat. Jen didn't think much of it, as at this particular moment she had a rush of customers, and she didn't pay the helpful one much mind.

Jen had had a pretty busy night, and she remembered cashing in her smaller bills for twenties so that she could replace the one-dollar bills back into the register to make change. She said she remembered having over one hundred dollars in twenties, but she wasn't sure how much more than that there was. When it came time to start preparing for the end of her shift, she looked at her tips one more time, and there were just several one-dollar bills and a five. She told me she was absolutely positive that the helpful guy had taken her tips. Jen was angry, with "asshole" and stronger cusswords flying out of her mouth at record speed.

I told her to count her bank, and that I would count the poker bank, and if the money didn't show up in either place, we could approach him. Jen was shaking with anger, ears too, as she quickly counted. Sure enough, the money wasn't there. When we went back out to the bar to confront Mr. Helpful, both he and Angel were gone. Jen's bunny tail bobbed left to right as she stomped from behind the bar and took a seat on a stool. "I can't believe he took advantage of me like that," she said. "I broke bread with that asshole. I mean, Marita, I bought him a drink, and then he steals from me. I don't know if I'm more angry or hurt."

Jen sat there contemplating her options, and then she made a decision. "I'm going to get my Goddamn money," she said. "He's staying with Angel, so I'm just going over there, and I'm going to get my money."

I wasn't sure if that was the best idea; it could be dangerous to provoke a man we didn't know. But Jen had no fear whatsoever. Jen was only about five-foot-four, and she was wearing bunny ears for Christ's sake. I tried very hard to discourage her from making the visit, but before I knew it, I was watching her little bunny tail bob up the street and into the distance. I was truly worried as I waited for her to return.

Meanwhile, J.W. regular Joe joined me at the bar for his morning spritzer. I gave him a brief account of the morning happenings with Mr. Helpful and our bunny. Just then, Jen marched back to the bar. "Something really strange is going on," she said." Angel's door is wide open, and there is no one there. I waited for a little while, but shit. I wanna get my money."

Jen sat back down at the bar and rehashed her woes. Working herself back into a frenzy, she decided, "Man, I'm going back up there to get my Goddamn money." And with that, she bobbed back up the street to Angel's house, even after Joe and I both tried once again to discourage her from confronting this guy away from the bar.

Maybe ten minutes went by before I spotted the ears flopping down the street back toward the bar. "Oh my God," I said as I saw Jen had two fists full of twenties. "I don't believe it. How on earth did you get it?" I asked.

"He was standing with his back to me working on the door," Jen explained. "I punched him right in the face and said, 'Give me my Goddamn money asshole.' Then he pulled all the money he had out of both of his pockets and told me I could have whatever he had. An asshole doesn't do that unless he took the Goddamn money in the first place." I just couldn't believe it.

"I tell you," Jen said. "You can spit on me, you can be an asshole to me, you can call me names," and as she spoke the next few words, her chin started to quiver and she started to cry. "But don't hurt my feelings." So that was it then. You can beat up a bunny, but you will feel her wrath if the feelings come into play. It was so sweet, I went around the bar and gave her a big hug. Jen was my new hero. Since that time, I've gotten to know Jen a lot better and very much enjoy her company. In fact, I found Jen and her boyfriend Max the perfect rescue dog for their lifestyle, and I don't give my rescue dogs to just anybody. Jen was a good bartender and a good person, and she worked at Johnny White's for many years while going to nursing school, later becoming an RN. It goes to show you, you really should never judge a bunny by its cover, or lack thereof.

19
Talk to the Man

To say J.W.'s was dog friendly would be an understatement. Most people who live in the Quarter have a dog or two, and almost all of J.W.'s regulars were among that crowd. Many of the customers' dogs even went to work with them at their respective jobs, and thus accompanied their owners to the bar later for after work cocktails. The dogs were just as happy to see one another as we were to see our friends. There are countless fascinating and loving stories about the dogs of Johnny White's; in fact, we even created the Johnny White's Sports Bar Canine Calendar, which was printed every year for a decade.

The bar's mascot, Little Johnny White, or J.W., was a very fun-loving dog that joined the bar when he turned just six weeks old. J.D. purchased him when another regular, Lisa, came in with his brother one day, showing off her new pup to the bar. The cute solid-white boxer pup tore at J.D.'s heartstrings, and before we knew it, here came J.W. That dog was definitely the most photographed dog in the French Quarter, perhaps the world. J.W. appeared in advertisements for the city before the Saints' football games. He was so often photographed by tourists that he learned to wait for the flash. J.W. loved to people watch, and when pretty girls approached the bar, he would throw his ball out into the street, so they would fetch it for him—over and over and over again. At our sister bar Mississippi River Bottom, J.W. became enamored with the white cue ball on the pool table. No other ball would do. It had to be the white cue ball. People would put it on the table for him, and he would box at it with his paws until the ball fell into the

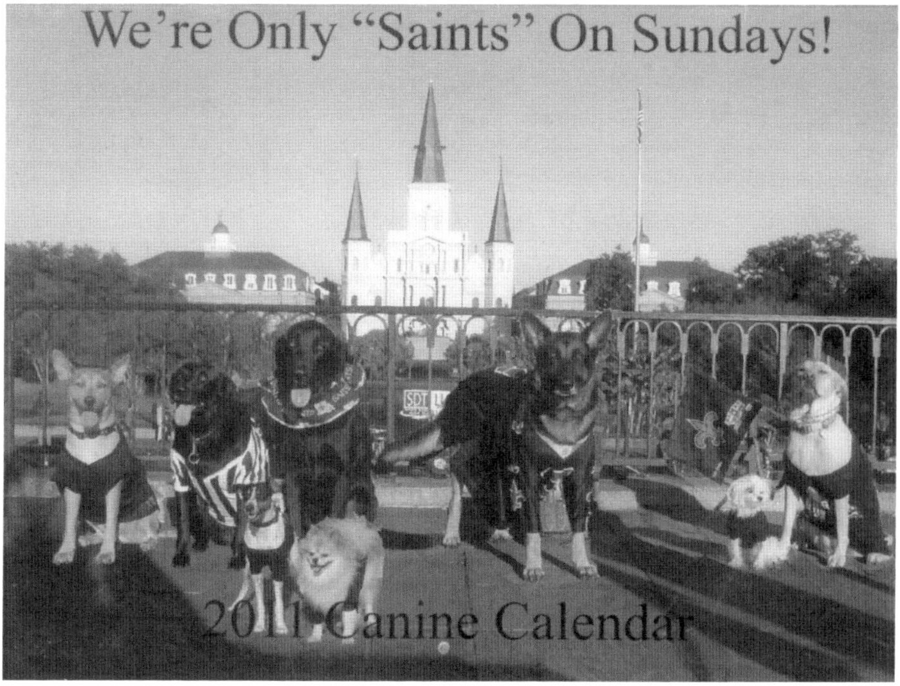

Cover of the 2011 Johnny White's Canine Calendar. *Author's collection.*

table's pockets, only stopping when he had worn everyone in the bar out. If the Mardi Gras videos and Katrina hadn't put Johnny White's on the map already, J.W. certainly was third runner-up. Everyone came year after year to see "the white dog" of the bar. J.W. passed away on November 6, 2014, after a life filled with fun and adventure. He is missed now just as much as the bar.

There are so many stories about the special dogs at this bar that they would fill the pages of another book. The following is just one very memorable story that illustrates the flavor of the importance of the bartenders' and customers' dogs and their lives at the bar.

The Steelers had just won the Super Bowl, February 2008. At Johnny White's Sports Bar, it was a big event. Paul, the employee who was responsible for cleaning the bar every morning, was in his element. Originally from Pittsburgh, Paul was a Steelers fan, and this was his special night. He took it upon himself to hold a special Steelers Super Bowl fest. The barbecue had been fired up on the Orleans side of the bar since early that afternoon. Manning his post, Paul was greeted by regulars popping in and out of the bar to grab some grub and a cocktail and give Paul their good luck blessings for the game. Paul's dog Lita Ford danced around his feet, keeping careful watch for the tiniest morsel to fall from the grill while Paul seasoned and flipped burgers, chicken and sausage.

Lita was a special little dog Paul had adopted when her previous owner found himself locked up in jail. Lita's breed is referred to as a min-pin, or miniature pinscher, but Lita was anything but miniature. She was plump both in size and in personality. Lita was at Paul's side throughout the Katrina storm, creating a real bond between the two. During the hurricane, Paul, Lita and bartender Marcie watched over the bar, and after Hurricane Katrina, Lita was considered one of the staff. She was the kind of companion to Paul that people mean when they say "A man and his dog."

Lita had a personality that often found Paul making compromises. "Okay, I'll put your favorite sweater on," he'd plead. "Then you'll go out in the rain, won't you?" Lita loved to be dressed. She hated having her nails clipped but loved to have them painted. She didn't look like a princess, but her actions told you that she was.

She loved her cookies handed to her in a small shot glass of milk. Perhaps this gave her a taste to things served in shot glasses; she used to lap up a popular shot known as Nuts and Berries, which is equal parts Bailey's, Frangelico and Chambord. Paul would let her have one of her own on occasion, and patrons would share theirs with her.

One night when she accompanied Paul to the bar, Lita found herself sharing one too many of these delicious milky concoctions. Paul noticed that Lia was acting a little funny, and then she made it clear that it was time to go home, barking and fussing at Paul. While she would have preferred to be carried, Paul was a firm believer in lying in the bed you've made. He told her to stiff it up and make the walk, all the time giggling at her swerving left and right in front of him, to make sure she didn't suffer anything more serious than a hangover

That was the day Lita gave up drinking. From that day on, she never had another sip of liquor. If only people were as smart as that. It usually takes years of drinking before we learn how to handle our liquor, and almost never do we just quit.

Anyway, this special little dog was a very large part of Paul's life, and having her present during the Super Bowl celebration was just a given.

I didn't make it to the bar that day, but as I arrived Monday morning at 7:00 a.m. for my usual entertaining shift, I was met at the door with frantic faces. Several of the regulars and the graveyard bartender had terror in their eyes and panic written on their faces. "Did you hear? Did you hear? We've

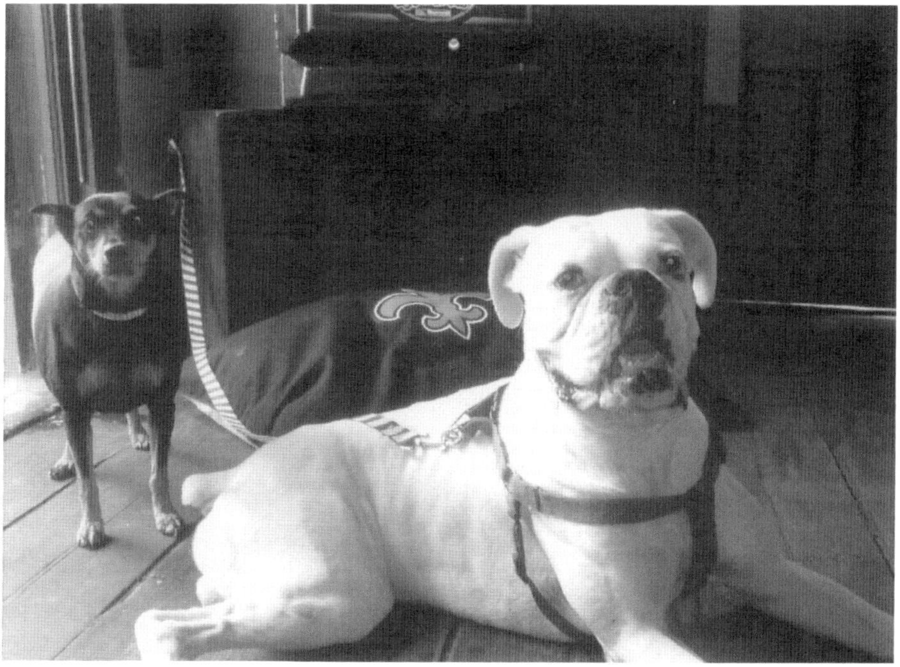

Lita Ford and J.W. posing for the Johnny White's Sports Bars Canine Calendar. *Author's collection.*

been looking all night!" A still drunk customer and Steelers fan, complete with a Roethlisberger jersey, Steelers beads and Koozie, hollered in my direction as I walked in the door.

"What?" I asked as I studied the scared, yet vacant faces, all lined up for me to question.

"Lita. Lita's gone," said Peter, the bartender on duty. "Marcie's been driving around all night with John Fox looking for her."

While everyone had been enjoying the celebrations the night before, Lita had just disappeared. The crowd at the bar had been so excited, celebrating, drinking, and then Paul felt a lump form in his throat the instant he realized Lita was no longer vacuuming the ground around the grill. He'd searched the bar, but she was nowhere to be found. He thought that someone might have scooped her up to "save" her. Or perhaps she started to walk home on her own, as she had a few times before, and got into some kind of trouble. Regardless, Paul was a mess.

It was a sea of input from all sides, and I began formulating a plan. First, I called the animal shelters in the neighborhood and made them aware she was missing. I called the little delis that were open twenty-four hours in the Quarter to ask if someone had found a dog. I knew we would find her, as much as I knew we had to find her for Paul's sake. In fact, it is difficult to explain the feeling I had when I found out the news. I was nervous and almost sick to my stomach, filled with anxiety and desperately trying to think of anything else I might have overlooked to help find our little Lita.

My back was turned to the bar as I stocked a few shelves to prepare for my shift. I glanced in the mirror, behind the liquor bottles, and noticed the dark silhouette of a man standing behind me. His hair was wavy and long, with a glow on the edges from the sun, resembling a silver lining. I stood there a moment motionless, wanting to collect my next plan of action.

As I finally turned to face him, Paul let out, "I'm leaving town". I already felt it—I knew that if he didn't find Lita, he really would leave the city. He very rarely let his hair down, but it was long and flowing and full. Paul normally came to work in shorts and a T-shirt that was sometimes torn, or dirty. He was there to clean our bathrooms and the floor and behind the bar. His appearance was the last thing on his mind. It was however, unusual to see Paul wearing anything but his work clothes. Today, he was dressed all in black. His long-sleeved button down shirt suited the look he was going for today. Paul was in mourning. A serious mourning, not to be taken lightly.

"I knew you were going to say that," I responded.

I tried to talk him down, giving my best at compassionate conversation and instilling hope that we would absolutely find her. I thought the best thing we could do right then was have a drink. I started to make Paul his usual Jameson and ginger ale, but he stopped me. He wanted to have a Nuts and Berries. I put the other drink aside, and started to make us two shots. As I put the shot in front of us, I looked at Paul and saw the emotions in his eyes. "Here's to finding our little girl," I said.

"You wanna go with me to talk to the man?" Paul asked.

I knew what he meant, even without explanation. He wanted to go pray at the St. Louis Cathedral. I said, "Sure." We just had to wait until I got off work at 11:00 a.m. and Marcie returned to go with us.

It wasn't long before Marcie walked into the bar, also beat up from the night before, solemn and upset that Paul was so down. We all had a round of Nuts and Berries as we reminisced about Lita.

We walked down Orleans toward the cathedral, silent and somber. I don't believe we spoke a word. It was a crisp and quiet day, not a soul in sight. I had only been to church a handful of times in my life before that day. I wasn't really sure what to expect, but it seemed like the right thing to do. In fact, it seemed like the only thing to do. When we made Jackson Square, the sun was shining down on us as if to wish us good luck.

Inside the cathedral corridor, a hall where you may light a candle for loved ones lost, was just as absent of any life as the town itself on this day. Not a caretaker in sight. At the door that allows entrance into the cathedral, Paul noticed, at breast height, a pillar with a dish, similar to a bird bath. It was holy water for anyone who wished to partake before entering the cathedral. Paul, as naturally as lighting a cigarette, placed his fingers in the bowl, scooped up what he could and sprinkled first Marcie, then me and lastly himself—clearing our way into the cathedral. We never spoke about it.

Paul made his way up to the altar. Marcie and I found refuge at seats halfway down the aisle. We watched as he walked onto the red-carpeted walkway that led up to the hearth. Paul knelt down on one knee and began to pray.

I watched him and thought about how special this moment was to me. While Paul, Marcie and I were deep in prayer, the St. Louis Cathedral's monsignor burst from the shadows and raced toward Paul in a terrifying frenzy. "You can't be up there!" he shouted, flailing his hands in consternation.

Unbeknownst to us, it was sacrilegious to cross the threshold to the altar. Apparently, I learned later, there is a wire that announces the presence of anyone uncouth enough to break the boundaries of this sanction.

Marcie and I were motionless as Paul pleaded with the monsignor. "Man, I'm praying here," he said. Red in the face, the monsignor made it extremely clear that we were no longer welcome in the cathedral. Speechless, embarrassed, appalled, the three of us walked down the aisle to exit the church. We followed Paul, who without speaking led us through Pierre Antoine Alley, to the back of the cathedral. At this time of day, there was no way into the garden. But Paul made it clear that he was not finished praying. Marcie and I stood watching as Paul scaled the fence into the garden. He calmly approached the statue in the garden known as Touchdown Jesus. (The statue's hands are raised above its head, in a gesture reminiscent of a referee at a football game announcing a score.) Paul took his time, and even though this was one of the most surreal moments I'd ever experienced, I was proud of him. After he scaled back over the fence and joined us, he seemed more at peace, like he believed it would work.

We parted ways with hugs. Not a half hour later, I received a phone call from Marcie with an update. Lita had been found. Apparently, she'd gotten tired of the party at the bar the night before and decided to make her own way home, when she happened upon another barbecue at the home of a couple of nice French Quarter residents. Lita decided to join them for dinner, and they kept her safe until the next morning, when they called the vet's number on her name tag. Paul had his heart and sidekick back. Lita joined him the next day to clean the bar as usual, and we did not take her presence there for granted.

20
Mints, Perfume, Something Else?

Pat O'Brien's is a New Orleans landmark bar, famous for its creation of the Hurricane, a rum cocktail that has become a New Orleans tradition. It's a large facility with several individual bars, each with its own personality. There are two smaller bars, one facing Toulouse known as the "locals' bar," and one facing Bourbon Street, as well as a wonderful dueling piano bar and a large festive outdoor courtyard.

In old-style tradition, the main bathrooms, both for men and women, feature a bathroom attendant who is at your beck and call, supplying guests with mints, perfume, mouth wash, hand lotion and other various toiletries, ensuring your visit to the facilities is all that it can be. In return, the attendant hopes for tips, as she, or he, gifts you with a towel to dry your hands. While I actually enjoy visiting a bathroom with all the extras, I always feel a little sorry for the attendant. Having to spend one's work day in a bathroom cannot be the most pleasant of jobs.

Our bathrooms at Johnny White's, on the other hand, were less than desirable. There were often no locks on the doors, so customers would have to keep one foot against the door to hold it shut while sitting on the throne to ensure privacy. Sometimes there would be soap in the dispenser, and occasionally, the facilities were equipped with paper towels as well, if you were lucky to catch it on the weekends. Our paper towel and toilet paper service arrived on Fridays, and Fridays only. In lieu of tips, guests often chose to dismantle the paper towel dispenser as their token of appreciation for using the facility, a gesture none of us have ever come to understand.

Paul, our janitor, had his job cut out for him on a daily basis, and the prime time to use the facilities at Johnny White's was always earlier in the day, just after Paul had cleaned. We painted the bathrooms twice in ten years, as guests also found it necessary to leave a message for their friends and others on the walls, some of which were very colorful. My favorite is a quick line that is written just outside the bathrooms, on the wall that led to the stairs. It read, "Go home dad, you're drunk!" There was one that was close to my heart in the ladies' room that read "Tip Marita Big!" I have no idea who left that, but it was touching.

For a time, a hole in the wall, created by some charming unknown character, allowed conversation between the men's and the ladies' rooms. While a trashcan was situated so as to block the hole, somehow it always found its way moved aside to amuse our visitors. I had heard there was a hole in the wall, but by the way people talked about it, it didn't sound significant. I seldom used the upstairs bathroom because employees had one of their own behind the bar, though it wasn't in much better shape.

When I eventually saw the magnitude of the hole, I was shocked. It was hard for me to believe that there wasn't more outrage, at least from the female guests. We had the hole fixed that very day, by quickly placing a square of plywood over the gap—it would have made any interior designer cringe.

When I first started working at Johnny White's I was going to make it my mission to upgrade our bathrooms. My goal was quickly shut down by the explanation that the state of the restrooms deterred people from lingering up there to have sex or do drugs. Thus, no locks on the doors. After working there for a while, I came to find that this policy actually made sense. On one slow New Orleans summer graveyard shift, Jen, the bartender on duty, who occasionally wore bunny ears, had just a few regulars in the bar. They were visiting together for several hours, and occasionally, a tourist would arrive, order a drink, use the facilities and leave with a smile on his face. It was pretty much an average shift—until, out of nowhere, a young, attractive and feminine black male crossdresser emerged from the stairwell that led to the bathrooms. He was one of Jen's occasional customers.

"Wait a minute," Jen hollered at him. "Where the hell did you come from?" A tourist who was on his fourth beer answered, "Oh, he's been up there for hours offering his services in the men's room." In other words, he was offering oral sex at a customer's request in exchange for a small tip.

In one split second it all came to Jen. That's why all those customers had left the bathroom with a smile on their faces. Some were probably just amused by the notion, and others may have partaken in the offer.

The crossdresser snuck in while Jen wasn't watching and spent hours up there taking post in the men's room. Jen was very upset and threw him out with a "and don't come back." She had always been nice to this person and was truly hurt that he had taken advantage of her in this way.

While I was mortified when I heard the story upon my arrival to take my shift, it was sort of amusing. For a short while, Johnny White's had had its own sort of bathroom attendant. Service with a smile.

21

Repelling Roaches

On yet another enlightening morning, this time about a year after Katrina, when we had regained some order to the bar, I was chatting with my morning men's group. We coined them the sewing circle: Saltwater Bob, because he's from Utah, also known as Louie; Gary, a cab driver, also known as Louie II; Bob Smith, also known as the Rev, because he has a paid for reverend's license; Perry, a fellow J.W. bartender at the time; and Joe.

The group of grumpy old men adopted our bar sometime after Katrina because one got thrown out of Harry's Corner, and they needed a new morning pub to frequent. The guys met at the bar every morning. Once a week, they gathered there and, after a few drinks, would pile in Bobby Smiths' car and head for Dorignac's, a grocery store in Metairie. They had a pact that once in the door, they each had fifteen minutes to get whatever it was on their respective lists. Then it was back to the sports bar.

Once a month, they followed another ritual, a trip to the barber. They always looked nicely coifed when they returned.

I looked forward to my sewing circle coming in about 9:00 a.m. They were a hoot. A couple of them had wives or longtime girlfriends who joined them, usually on their second trip to the bar a little later in the morning or early afternoon. The group was gruff and prone to pick on one another, poking fun at their shortcomings. Most of them were retired, really stand-up guys. J.D. had so much fun with them that he had joined the group. All of them, including J.D., went on an annual fishing trip together. They'd argue the entire time, playing cards and betting on anything imaginable. They cooked and fished and really enjoyed themselves.

These guys bet on golf, baseball, horse racing, you name it, but once they took it a bit too far. A flash of misbegotten inspiration led to the creation of the death pool, betting on which of our French Quarter cast of characters would bite the bullet first. Luckily, the death pool didn't last too long; it wasn't as funny as they thought it was to most of us, and it fizzled out due to several comments of it being in bad taste.

I started to really look forward to betting on horses every Thursday with the guys. J.D. would take bets, and we'd all pass money around. Generally, everyone would pretty much end up with what they'd started with.

One morning, I overheard Joe tell Bobby that he gave "that asshole Vince a five-spot yesterday." I almost came out of my shoes. Vince was a low-life, sleazy street hustler whom I had eighty-sixed from the bar a couple of weeks before for stealing money from a regular. Vince had been making a nuisance of himself for a while before I finally told him off for stealing money off the bar, B-drinking (trying to charm drinks out of other customers) and hustling customers.

"Joe! I just told you last week never to give Vince money or anything for that matter. I pointed him out to you." I was furious. I had explained in detail to Joe all the things Vince had done and exactly how angry I was at this guy.

Apparently, Joe had been at Mississippi River Bottom (MRB) having a wine spritzer for brunch when Vince walked in. Vince cozied in next to Joe, recognizing him as a J.W.'s regular, and started small chitchat. Joe, aware of Vince's M.O., was expecting the worst. Then it hit: "Man, can you spot me a five for a couple of days? Just need to get some smokes."

Joe pulled out a five and amiably handed it to Vince. And sure enough, Vince was on his way. And Joe hasn't seen him since.

"Joe, how could you?" I cried. "Do you feel pressured by this guy? Do you actually like the guy?" Joe tried to interrupt, but I was on an angry roll. "I just don't understand it, Joe." I shook my head in disgust.

"You done?" Joe asked of me. I nodded yes. Quietly. "Listen, Marita," he said. "If you'd just shut up a minute I'll explain it to you." The Rev nodded as if he already understood.

"I got off easy." Joe said.

"What!" I was appalled.

"Just listen! Sometimes it costs you twenty dollars, sometimes ten."

"Sometimes a whole lot more," Bob Smith chimed in.

"Yea, but it only cost me a five-spot," Joe continued. "You see those guys come around and ask you for a donation, basically—that you know in advance you will never see again. However, with that donation, you are buying something. You are buying your peace. After they get their donation, they will do anything and everything to avoid you, so they don't have to pay you back. If they see me sitting in a bar, they will slink by as unnoticed as possible. Watch, I won't see Vince again for a very, very long time.

"After they get their donation, they're gone. I don't have to entertain the ridiculous small talk they blabber in hopes of getting a drink, or cash. It's almost magical—they just disappear and avoid you at all costs, moving around you invisibly."

It was an epiphany. That had never occurred to me. Rather than putting up with these cockroaches who were sneaking around every corner, ready to cling to anyone who'd put up with them, you could just buy their absence. In the future, all that is necessary to make them skedaddle at their own free will is to "loan" them a smidgen of money, and it will automatically repel them.

Brilliant, really. I could go about my business, and the leeches of the Quarter would orbit around me and never touch down. Wow.

I sat down and sipped a swirl of my wine spritzer with seven and thanked Joe and the Rev for the lesson.

22

The Memory Pill

Often in the mornings, the bar was occupied only by a group of men we coined the sewing circle. Saltwater Bob, Joe, the Rev (Bob Smith) and J.D. were ribbing Louis II (Gary) because his wife had researched a fascinating pill she felt sure Gary should take. Gary's wife, Liz, was always researching things and dedicating any particular moment to enforcing whichever particular contraption or medication happened to be the one that seemed to be important at the time.

Liz had purchased herself and Gary super-duper tennis shoes that were sworn to relieve back pain, increase energy and probably leap tall buildings in a single bound as well. When Gary went to the doctor, however, he mentioned the shoes to get his physician's opinion of them, only to have the doctor explain that they were good shoes, and good shoes are important, but they were not the miracle shoes Liz and Gary had been hoping for, at $600 a pair.

Liz was a good researcher, however. She possessed every contraption advertised on late-night infomercials, and pretty much everything she purchased did what it was supposed to do. The Vegomatic, the 2,001-purpose paper cutter, the supersonic telephone system with twenty extra features, and the list goes on. On this particular day, however, the sewing circle was discussing Gary's new memory pills. The pills that Liz had acquired for Gary had all kinds of herbs and minerals that were meant to stimulate the part of the brain that helps retain information. Gary had been taking the pills for almost a week, and all the ribbing aside, he felt that they might actually be doing the trick. It was hard to tell, but apparently, Gary felt a little more knowledgeable about past events and gathered information.

J.D. was finished with his morning tasks at the bar, and it was time to start betting on the races. Joe was not a big better, and he often called a cab upon leaving the bar to go home for his nap if the Rev was not taking him home. However, on this particular occasion, Gary was planning on leaving the bar fairly soon and offered to swing back around and pick up Joe, if he waited on the corner by the bar. As Gary left to get his cab, Joe finished his wine spritzer and started to make his way outside to the corner. I got a couple more Miller Lights out of the cooler and gave them to the Bobs as we all chose a few horses to bet on for the next race. I was stuck on the five horse in every race. It was a system that seemed to work for me at least one-tenth of the time. After the first race, I noticed J.D. looking out the window at something as I handed him two dollars for my next bet. I joined his gaze out the window to see Joe still standing there on the corner.

After the fourth race, I made my way around the bar to pick up a few cans left by the poker machine by past customers. As I walked by the window, I noticed that Joe was still standing there on the corner. "Man, it's taking Gary a long time," I said to the boys. Everyone agreed that poor Joe had been standing there for an exceptionally long time, waiting on his friend to scoop him up.

Just after I handed over my next two dollars for the sixth race, I decided to poke my head out and check on Joe. Joe was on the phone and walking toward me. "Idiot," he said into the phone. "Goddamn memory pills, my ass." Joe closed his phone. "Call me a cab would you, hon?" Joe requested. "Memory pills must not have kicked in yet." We laughed and jabbed at Gary until the cab got there. By next week's sewing circle gathering, Gary was off the memory pills.

23

What Time Is Four O'clock Football?

What time is Four O'clock Football? customers would ask, poking their heads into the bar, making sure not to miss the graveyard shift's latest craze. I would usually tilt my head at them to illustrate how ludicrous their question was. One of our graveyard shift bartenders, Peter, came to the bar recruiting for the new football league. Peter was also known as Peter Jesus, referencing the way his hair and beard gave him an uncanny resemblance to the one and only. On this particular day, Peter was recruiting players to join his Four O'clock Football team—4:00 a.m., that is. Other times, Peter would recruit referees, cheerleaders and even spectators.

The minute I heard the idea, it sounded fun and very French Quarter fabulous, but I never dreamed it would go on for so many seasons. I figured everyone would show up, or not, for a few games, and the idea would fizzle out. However, the enthusiasm that Peter brought to the game generated excitement not just from our bar but late-night bars throughout the Quarter.

Several of our bar's regulars, bartenders and regulars from other bars would congregate every Wednesday night/Thursday morning for a friendly yet competitive game. The teams primarily consisted of a standing match between Johnny White's bartenders and customers versus Tropical Isle bartenders and regulars. Tourists were often recruited to join in the fun, and it ended up being a definite highlight of their trip. Played just outside the bar, on Bourbon Street, the games lasted for one hour with a fifteen-minute half-time intermission—just enough time to grab a quick drink. The game

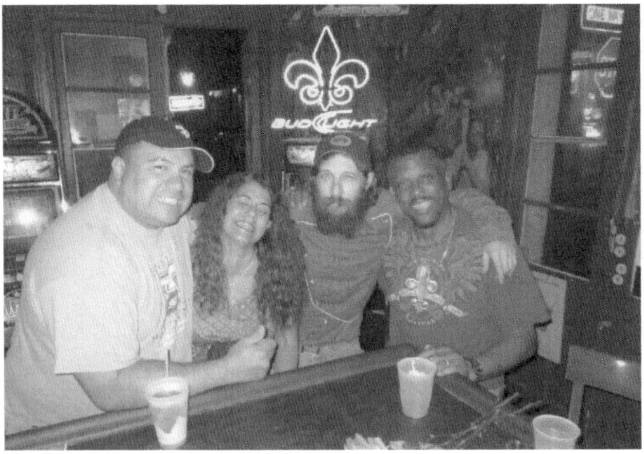

Bartender Peter, pictured third from the left, recruiting for his 4:00 a.m. football league. *Author's collection.*

was quite dangerous for the players, as it was full-contact and they were playing on asphalt.

I had to be at the bar at 7:00 a.m. on Thursdays for my shift. As enticing as the idea of the game was to me, making it there even as a spectator was neither reasonable nor responsible. However, Peter was usually still at the bar in the mornings when I arrived for work. He would fill me in on all the details of the game, play by play. It was fascinating to me how he would recall the intricacies of what went down.

Often Peter was covered in bruises and wounds from asphalt scrapes or worse. One morning, he showed me a serious injury on his stomach from running into one of the poles that frame our sidewalks. Ornate, with metal horse heads, the poles had been installed for tethering horses when the French Quarter was established in the 1700s. They were not fun to run into at full speed. Other members of the teams were often sprawled about the bar mending their wounds as well. It was an interesting scene to walk into every Thursday morning.

After the event took off, and people showed up for game after game, players decided that there had to be a championship game at the end of each season. They decided to hold it on Ash Wednesday. So, the season lasted a full year and ended with our version of a Super Bowl, coined the Ash Bowl.

The trophy was priceless. On top of a bar ashtray was a football suspended with various items found around the bar, all glued together and placed on top of the liquor shelf.

It wasn't until Ash Wednesday 2012 that I finally mustered up enough energy to get up and walk down to the bar for the 4:00 a.m. game. All

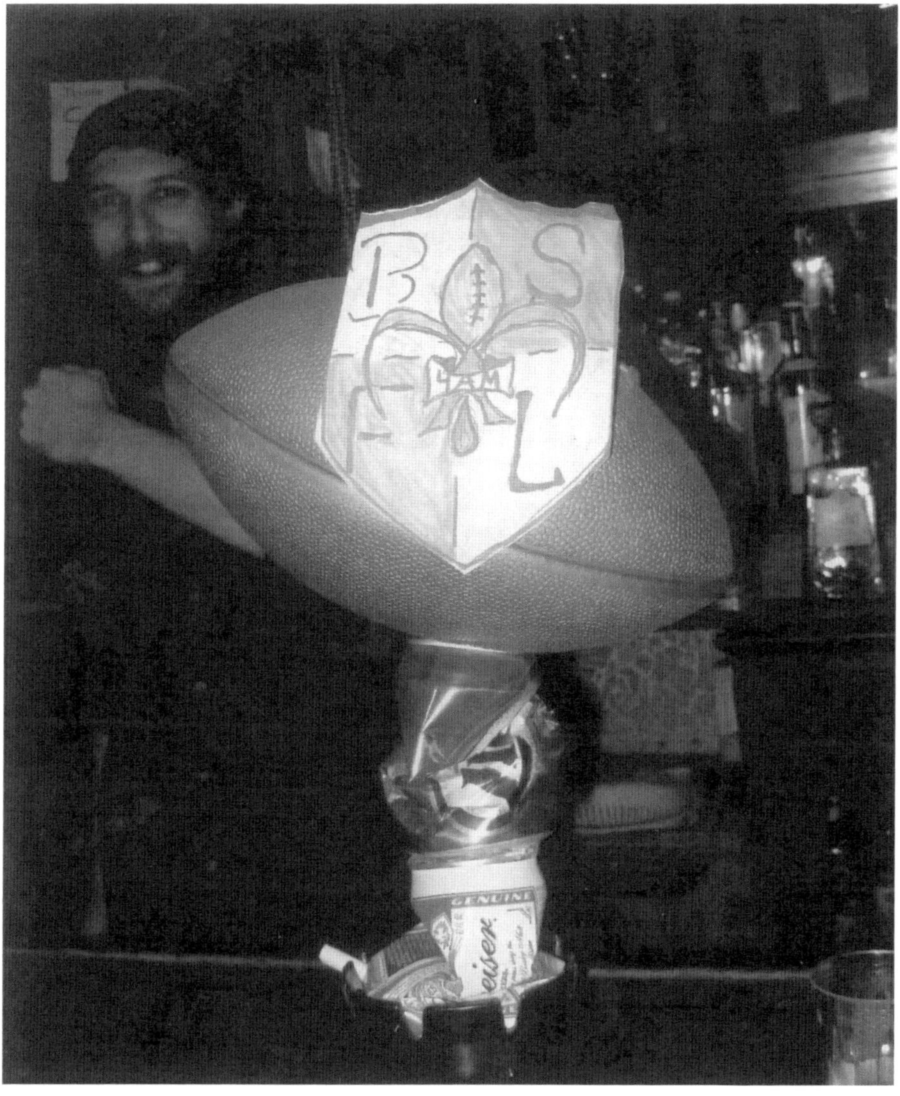

Four O'clock Football Ash Bowl Trophy. *Ken Scott.*

the hype that had surrounded the sport for several seasons now had really built the event up in my mind. Jen, who also worked graveyard shifts, even had special cheerleading outfits made up for several of the bartenders who frequented the bar on game nights.

It was drizzling the evening that I attended. Some customers of Peter's from Florida made a special trip to be in the city just for the Ash Bowl. I arrived as Peter was asking people to get a drink and join him in the street. I pulled a little barstool outside, grabbed a cup of coffee and watched with much anticipation.

In just moments, the first person went for a long pass and hit the pavement with ultra-zest. Glasses flying, head hitting pavement and ball coming loose, it was painful to watch. Shortly thereafter, another pass was thrown, and an opposing player made the catch but fell backward. Head hitting curb, back to pavement, left hand catching was scraped, good and bloody. And they wanted to know if I would be playing? Yeah, right. But now I could visualize just how all those bruises and cuts I watched them nurse every Thursday morning were created.

My favorite story of Four O'clock Football happened in 2010, when the pro basketball all-star game was held in New Orleans. It was a big deal to have it here, and the city was filled with visitors attending the events. We were lucky enough to have the commentary for the game filmed above our bar at Johnny White's Bar and Grill. Charles Barkley and Magic Johnson were just a couple of the celebrities who were handling the event. The filming went on for several days, requiring that a few film trucks be stationed around the bar to house the lighting and camera equipment. The trucks were there for twenty-four hours, so security was required around the clock as well.

When it was time for the standing Wednesday night Four O'clock Football game, the security guard assigned by the film crew that night stood by the truck on the corner of Orleans and Bourbon and watched the game develop before his eyes. About a half hour into the game, a tourist walked down Bourbon and happened upon the group in the street. He made his way over

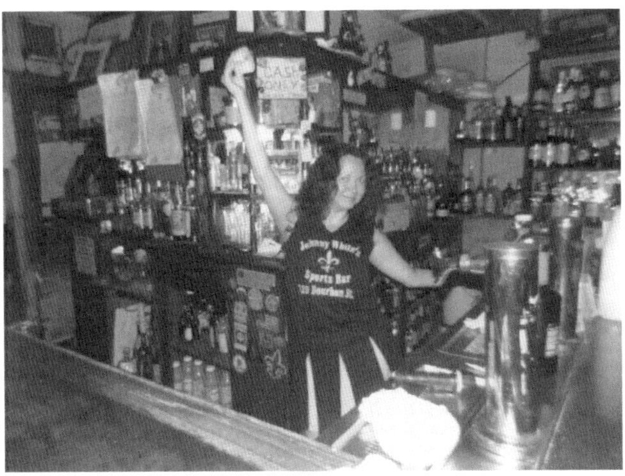

Bartender Jennifer in her Four O'clock Football cheerleading outfit. *Zach A. Lbarran.*

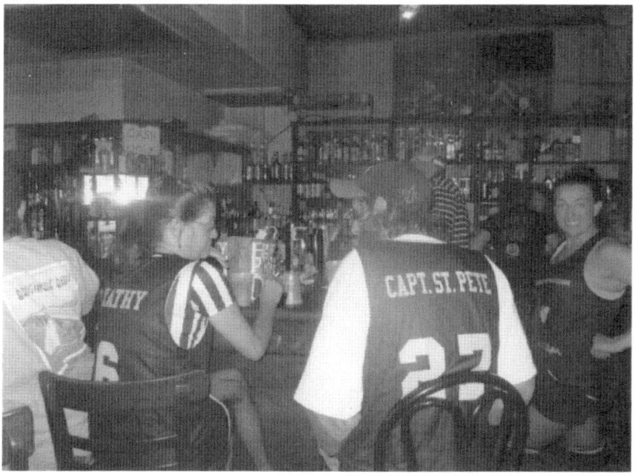

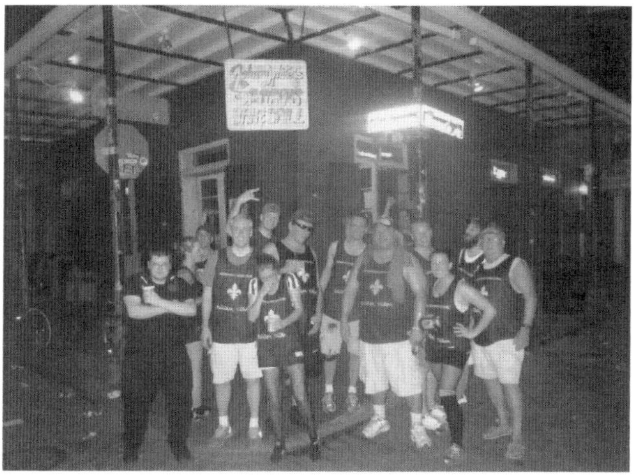

Top: Four O'clock Football player Kathy discussing plays with team quarterback Peter. *Zach A. Lbarran.*

Bottom: Johnny White's Four O'clock Football team. *Zach A. Lbarran.*

to the security guard. Apparently, he stood there for a moment and then inquisitively asked the security guard, standing at post in full gear, "Hey man, what are you security for?"

The security guard answered without hesitation, "For the game."

The tourist stood there observing for a moment. He gazed at the eight unruly looking characters frolicking and rolling on Bourbon Street. "For that game?" he asked, amazed.

24

Johnny White's Survivor and Fun with the Phone

The beginning of the morning shift at J.W.'s was one of the more challenging moments of the day at the bar. My day would often start with the bar filled with customers who should have left hours ago. People who only came out for the graveyard shift would annoy the morning sewing circle with their late night–style rhetoric. Barflies falling asleep on their stools would try their best to pretend they were focused, shaking their heads and slapping their faces to bring consciousness back. It was always a bear to walk in on, and while we all sympathize with the graveyard bartender's clientele, as the ultimate goal was to have a good ring on the cash register, we surely appreciated when they cleaned up the scene at the bar before we arrived for the 7:00 a.m. shift.

On one very cold late November morning, the bar had several graveyard customers still sipping their watered down drinks, trying to charm new customers as they arrived. A lovely young couple came in, announcing they had just moved to the Quarter part-time. The gentleman was a scriptwriter and his wife a designer, both from Norway. They spoke excellent English, and as we were trying to get to know one another, three graveyard drinkers desperately wanted to engage in the conversation. Barely able to form sentences, one would start a new conversation where the other left off. I was trying to be polite, but I could tell my new customers were less than thrilled with the situation.

After having asked the graveyard drinkers to politely mind their own business several times, we had all had it with them. Then, I had an idea.

Rather than ask them to leave and cause a scene, I thought of a way to get these graveyard-shifters to ask themselves to leave. Everyone in the bar would play "Johnny White's Survivor," and one by one the people who should have left hours ago would vote themselves out of the bar. It was really kind of brilliant. We laughed and had fun with it, and something amazing transpired. We found that the customers, regulars, who we used to have trouble getting to go home—people we would have to ask over and over again to pick up their belongings and finally get out the door—took Johnny White's Survivor seriously. It was remarkable. We would just say, "It's time to play—Johnny White's Survivor," and the graveyard drinkers would start collecting their things. Perhaps it was because it was always a unanimous decision that caused their exit, or maybe it was because they were so used to winning time and time again, but it never took long to clear the bar with this simple game.

One of our regulars, Freddie, a musician on Bourbon Street, came to the bar almost nightly and often took power naps after hours of playing the jukebox. It was not uncommon to find Freddie sleeping at the bar upon my arrival at 7:00 a.m. He was a charming guy, and it was a compliment that we made him feel so comfortable at J.W.'s that it was his home away from home, but at seven o'clock in the morning, the last thing I wanted to do was wake Freddie up and beg him to go home. However, one word about Johnny White Survivor and Freddie was packed up and out the door. He wasn't happy about it, mind you, but nonetheless, he respected the rules.

One of our regulars, James from Ohio, sometimes came in right before the morning shift just to watch Survivor take place. Many people got a huge kick out of it, and it truly turned what had been an impossible situation into a fun-loving sport.

Yet another Johnny White's game was created once we realized that we somehow scored the phone number for the pay phone across the street. Fun with the Phone was a game we would play on long summer days to amuse ourselves and our customers. J.D. would take several napkins folded up, place one single dollar bill on top of them, and then stuff it all into an envelope. At quick glance, it appeared to be a wad of money. J.D. would then sneak the envelope between the top of the payphone and the box that held the payphone. It was not easy to see if you weren't looking for it.

We would then call the payphone and wait for an unsuspecting tourist to answer, timing the ringing with people we saw walking by we thought might be fun suspects. When someone answered, one of us would tell the person,

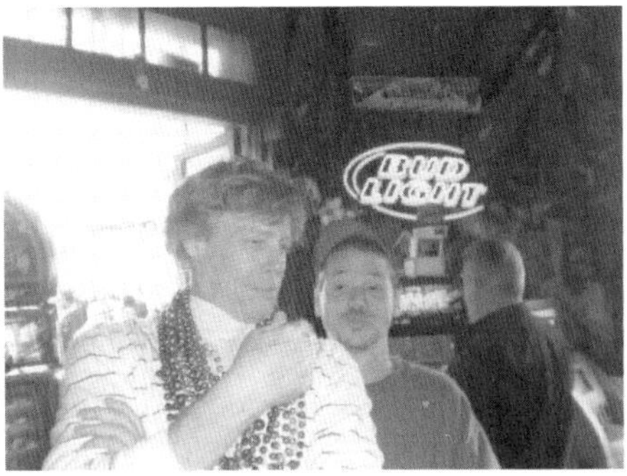

J.W.'s regular Lou breaking the news to regular Freddie that he has just been voted out of the bar during a game of Johnny White's Survivor. *Zach A. Lbarran.*

"Look, I left the money. But you tell Bob this is the last time. I'm just not doing it anymore! See it? It's in an envelope on top of the phone." The person would slide the envelope out, and what happened next was always fun to watch. Some people just took the envelope, put the phone down and walked away. A few honest souls gently tucked the envelope back on top of the phone, hung up and left. One particularly memorable guy snatched the envelope and ran down the street. The especially observant would open the envelope, see the one-dollar bill with the napkins and laugh.

It was good fun.

One day, a port-a-potty arrived across the street in front of Tropical Isle. It was locked shut with a heavy chain. I called the pay phone as a woman was walking by. When she answered, I said, distraught, "Oh, thank goodness you answered. My boyfriend thought it would be funny and he has locked me in this port-a-potty. Do you see me? I'm right across the street," She said yes, but then was unsure whether to believe me or not. She made me promise that I was telling the truth. Then she politely agreed to help me and walked over to the port-a-potty and looked in through the peephole. We all laughed, and then I went outside to greet her. She was a good sport.

We played jokes on all different kinds of people with that phone, including a policeman whom I hadn't noticed standing nearby. At first, I almost hung up the phone when he picked it up, but when he answered the phone by saying, "Joe's Abortion Clinic, you make 'em, we scrape 'em," I knew I had a fellow jokester on the line. I gave it my all. In an Indian accent, I said, "Sir, can I please speak to your manager?" He tried to explain to me that he was talking on a pay phone, but I pretended not to understand and was persistent that I must speak to his manager or the owner. He was getting visibly irritated, using hand gestures now, and we all started to laugh loud enough for him to hear. We waved at him, me still on the phone. He was lovely and came over to meet us. Those were the days.

25

Rock Stars

It was my birthday, and I was feeling especially happy this day. The weather was perfect. All doors to the sports bar were open, creating a beautiful breeze through the bar. A nice flow of tourists filled the streets, and business was steady. I had just reopened my vampire shop in a new location at the corner of Orleans and Royal, just down the road from the bar. It was an exciting time in general. I was serving up some drinks when a couple escaped out of their cab from what appeared to be a grueling experience by the exasperation in their expressions. They were each lugging elegant leather backpacks, hers a light pink, his a deeper blue. They looked expensive and stuck out, as I'd never seen leather backpacks before.

They were both in their early thirties. He was bald with a tremendous sense of confidence he wore almost like a suit. His wife, or at least that's how she was introduced to us, was okay looking, basically an average brunette, who was now beaming from ear to ear.

"Oh, we are so glad to finally be here." The couple quickly explained that their luggage had been lost and all they had were their backpacks. They ordered some drinks and offered to include one for me in the round. I immediately had a funny feeling about them, but I couldn't put my finger on what it was. They said they were from Vegas, and that it was her first time in the city, but he had been several times, and all of a sudden, I remembered him. He had been in the bar about six to eight months ago, telling us some fantastical stories about how much money he spent saving the life of his very sick mastiff dog. I remembered that his story had seemed a bit farfetched, although at the time, I couldn't remember the entire tale. He, however, confirmed the story, and she joined right in, making his original story much more believable to me. I felt a little bad I had doubted him.

He then confided in me that he had been the lead singer of Nickelback, a popular alternative rock band. However, fame was just not for him, so he left the group, which disbanded, and he started a computer career in Las Vegas. Currently, he said, he was head of the technology department for the famous Bellagio Hotel—one of my favorites. I always visited the Bellagio when I was in Vegas to grab a glass of wine overlooking their water show in the ponds at the front of the hotel. He threw in, "Hey, I will throw you a hotel comp before I leave." He then proceeded to play the same Nickelback song on the jukebox six times. They were different versions of the song, and he was having fun explaining the different nuances in each version. I personally was tired of the song. But his wife humored him and said that he did miss the music business a bit. They talked about their mansion in Vegas and the fact that this was her last hurrah before a grueling time ahead. It seemed their good friend Wesley Snipes had given her a lead role in the fourth Blade film.

She went on to explain that she had to lose a great deal of weight. Even though she was not in bad shape, she was not in great shape, so I could see that she would have to lose a few pounds, but the means she went on to describe seemed more than drastic. She was to undergo extreme liposuction and a six-week training program. Then they would break her jaw and fix her teeth.

It seemed very extreme, and I sincerely felt sorry for her. I even took time to write down a healthy diet and exercise program for her in lieu of having to go through liposuction. But she insisted that she had procrastinated too long, and there simply was no other option if she wanted the role. She was trying to hook me, so she also told me that their good friend Wesley Snipes had pretty much put all of their friends in the film, and God damn it, it worked. I resisted for several hours, but then finally the little nagging desire to be in the film had me asking her if it could be a possibility to secure a small role for myself. She asked her husband, and he said sure! If only I had realized at that point that the *Blade* series had been a trilogy, it might have alerted us to what was ahead. I suppose they chose *Blade* because they knew I had just reopened my vampire shop.

J.D. entered the bar to do the banks, and I introduced him to my new friends. They immediately flaunted their wealth at J.D. with stories about the man's fame and elaborate position at the Bellagio. J.D. perked up at the Vegas connection. Then, when we were both hooked, the husband played his card. Expressing irritation at the situation they found themselves in, they explained that they were making arrangements to have his assistant wire them money, as their credit cards were in the lost luggage. All they had with them now were a few hundred dollars in bills and a checkbook the wife had stashed in her backpack.

They bought another round and insisted on including J.D., explaining that they had to leave the bar soon to go handle their money matter, even though they would much rather just hang out at the bar all day. They were thinking of ordering something for lunch. Playing it perfectly casual, the husband slid in, "You wouldn't cash a check would you?" laughing a little, like it was a ridiculous idea.

J.D. generously asked, "How much you need?" Of course, he wanted to help this friendly couple out, but he was also thinking about his Vegas connection.

Now, here's where the husband had to be careful. Don't ask for too much to scare J.D. off, yet ask for enough to make this all worthwhile. "Well, we should have our wired money by tomorrow for sure, so it's only one day. How about $500?"

"Sure, no problem," J.D. offered, and the "wife" wrote out the check. I didn't get a look at it at this time, but why would I? They decided to relax and order in lunch, and when they found out it was my birthday, they insisted on buying me lunch as well—with J.D.'s money.

The following day, I arrived at the bar at 7:00 a.m., and the mysterious couple followed me in. It turned out that their tickets were not sorted yet and they would be forced to stay another day. They also told me because they knew I had just reopened my boutique, that as a small token of their appreciation for my hospitality toward them, they had instructed their assistant to order a gift certificate for me from Staples for $500, as they knew that I would be needing supplies. Boy, how I wanted that to be true. They weren't sure where to send it, so they just made arrangements for it to be mailed to the bar, so I should watch for it. Like a widow waiting for her husband's lost ship at sea.

That day, the stories went on and on, and the more fantastical they became, somehow the more believable they seemed. It was a strange phenomenon. As I look back now, it seemed he was teaching his partner how to make their stories work. He would tell one, as an example, and then sit back and let her take the reins. Pretty industrious really. They spun a story about having purchased a large blue skeleton at the tourist trinket shop a few doors down. She said it was for the room in their house they called "The Dungeon." She said they had their assistant call in and pay for it over the phone. To this day, every time I walk past it, I cringe a little.

A little voice kept whispering suspicions to me. So finally, that evening, after a long day and night out, I got on my computer and looked up Nickelback, only to find that this guy looked *nothing* like anyone in the band and it seemed they were still touring and performing. The husband had told me the band dismantled when he left, as it was *his* band. I was not surprised, but I was angry. It was too late to call J.D., so I decided I would call him as soon as I got to the bar in the morning—and so I did.

J.D. also didn't seem that surprised, but he told me he had cashed another check for them for $300 before he left the bar the night before—money he would never see again. He told me their check was under the register drawer. This was the first time I had the opportunity to see that the check was from a karate studio in Florida. I called the number and was not surprised to find that it had been disconnected.

The couple was supposed to leave early this morning for Las Vegas, if that's even where they came from. Well, lo and behold, I suppose they didn't want to let go of their cash cow yet, so here they strolled in the door. I was fuming mad inside, and anxiety filled my stomach at the opportunity they had just presented us. He ordered two Bloody Marys, and when he put the money on the bar, I saw he still had a wad of bills. I pretended to be thrilled to see them and put them off for a minute when I went to the back to call J.D. I told him they had just walked in and that he still had some of J.D's loot, so that J.D. should get over here right away. I put the phone down and quickly went back to entertain them until J.D. got there. They now seemed so transparent to me, and I wanted to confront them more than anything. But I didn't want to blow our chance, so I had to smile at all the lies that came flowing.

As I was listening to more bullshit, I saw J.D.'s truck appear behind them through the window. I told the husband that J.D. was here, and he should go out to talk to him. He didn't hesitate, leaving me to keep the wife entertained. I wanted to smack her right in the face. Still, their lies were pretty good, and I still secretly hoped that Staples gift certificate would arrive one day.

The husband came in, quickly picked up their backpacks and said to his wife, "We got to go, come on."

I said, "Leaving in such a hurry?" He just gave me a look, and they headed out the door farthest away from J.D.

J.D. walked in with a look of disgust on his face. I don't know if it was directed at them, at me or at himself, or maybe all three.

"So, you got some of your money back?" I knew he had.

"No," he said matter-of-factly. "But now I got two weeks at the Bellagio for ten people." If I had had a sip of anything in my mouth at the time I would have spit it out.

"What? I know you didn't believe that shit!"

"No, not really. But I want it to be true." I knew exactly what he had meant.

J.D. and I sat around for a few hours contemplating our stupidity and gullibility. He told me it was a lesson learned and a story we would laugh about for a long time. I felt bad that he lost his money, but he was right. It was an $800 story we would share for the rest of our lives.

About a year later, I was making coffee at 7:15 a.m. when a group of around seven guys entered the bar. One had long curly hair, one with dreadlocks, one with unruly hair and long beard, one with short spikey hair, two with kind of a preppy look and one was bald. They entered the bar in a row and all sat down one next to the other, all looking at me in anticipation. I couldn't help myself. "Are you guys a band?" If they weren't, they should have been. They politely laughed and said that they weren't, but they could see why I might have thought that. I made them all drinks, and then a little lightbulb went off in my head. I thought I could really make J.D. laugh with this one.

I filled the guys in on what had happened to us with the rock star couple and told the guys I wanted them to pretend they were a band—someone like Nickelback—not too famous, but famous enough so that the name would be recognizable. They came up with Phish, which was perfect! I told them about J.D.'s music club on Frenchman Street, the Blue Nile. The plan was that they were here to perform at the House of Blues, but because I treated them so well, and they liked the bar, that they would do me a huge favor. If J.D. wanted them to, they would head over to the Blue Nile after they had finished their concert to do a few songs onstage for us. I told them when we had J.D. completely fooled, I wanted one of them to say, "We are more than happy to do this for you, if you'll do us one favor?" I wanted him then to say, "Our luggage got lost on the plane, and we don't have much cash. Would you be able to cash a check for us?" I thought that would be a hilarious punch line, J.D. would get a good laugh out of it and we would come clean.

Well, I called J.D. and preempted the story, setting my band up for success. The excitement in my voice had J.D. equally excited that the Blue Nile might be in for a nice treat that night. When J.D. showed up, I introduced them, and he was polite but excused himself and went to the office. He was taking a little too long, so I went back to see what was keeping him. I found him looking through our local music paper. "I don't see Phish listed as being in town at all." Perhaps he really had learned a lesson after last time. I pretended to be annoyed. "Oh, for Christ's sake, J.D., come out here and meet the band. They're doing us a huge favor." So, he followed me.

They talked for a while, and the guys were charming. When J.D. said, "Well, I sure would appreciate you guys coming over for a little while tonight," we knew we had him. I winked at my band leader. He said his lines perfectly. However, much to my chagrin, instead of getting the joke, the guys seemed to have appealed to J.D.'s generous nature. "Well, how much ya need?" J.D. asked.

I just looked at him, and we all busted out laughing. "Guess you didn't learn your lesson after all!" I told him.

"Well, y'all really look like a band!" he answered. Moral of the story is, if you happen to be in New Orleans, are a little short on cash and look like you might be a rock star, you might want to stop by and see J.D.

26

Last Call

There was nothing easy about last call at Johnny White's. We seemed to count down the years as they started to slip away from us, and as we got closer to the day we would lose our lease, we all shared a certain anxiety. J.D. had originally secured a twenty-three-year lease, and while we were hopeful that it would be renewed, as time grew closer, we found out that the White family had plans of its own for the corner bar. They planned to renovate and open it under their own umbrella of Johnny White locations. Grabbing at straws, every now and then one of the bartenders and even occasionally, a customer, would come up with a haphazard idea to help save the bar. However, rightfully so, the White family wished to reclaim that section of the building, making our efforts futile.

We had various expectations for our last hurrah. We hired a second line band that would lead our march from J.W.'s at midnight to our sister bar MRB on St. Philip. Most of us couldn't really imagine what this time would be like because we didn't want to picture it. I remember on several occasions when the topic was brought up, someone would quickly raise a beer and change the topic. However, over the last year at J.W.'s, we made sure all of our regulars and regular tourists were aware of our last day. People, throughout the year, made their plans to be there, securing hotel and travel arrangements and checking in with us now and then to see if any plans had been changed. While we wanted to plan activities for our last party, it was difficult to get excited.

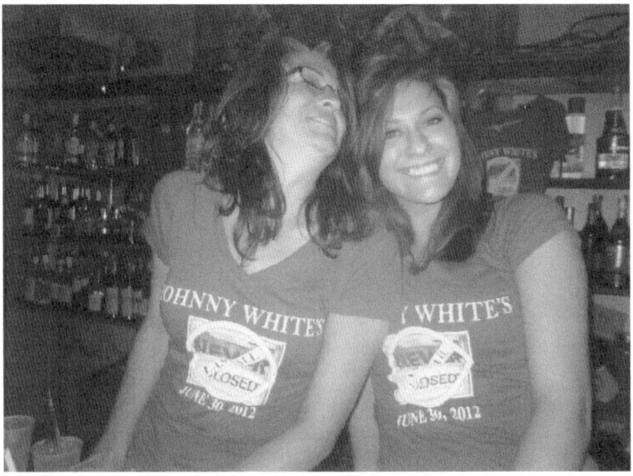

J.W. regulars sporting the bar's special edition "Last Call" T-shirts. *Zach A. Lbarran.*

In New Orleans tradition, saying goodbye is celebrated as much as any other event. Rather than mourning those lost, those in the city celebrate the life of the deceased. Usually, immediately after the service, a second line band follows the body in a funeral buggy to the grave site. A *second line* refers to the group of people following the first line, which consists of a brass band and those who are throwing the event. Handkerchiefs and parasols are held high while second liners dance in the street, celebrating their loved one passed. While we had special T-shirts made and knew our last weekend party would spill into the streets, there was such a sour taste in our stomachs during the time, it was anything but enjoyable.

Then it was upon us. Johnny White's last call. J.D. had taken out a page in our local *Gambit* news rag. It was a farewell letter from him to the bar.

Johnny White's Sports Bar
Last Call

Sadly, the day is rapidly approaching when those dreaded words, words that were never spoken for 23 years, will be heard…Last Call!

The stupid little bar on the corner of Bourbon and Orleans will be closing at months end.

I thought it would be easy to let her go—extra time off to enjoy life and travel. After all wasn't she a whore, always wanting money for this and that. Often times being stressed out and dealing with her attitude. She never closed, and often would call me at three in the morning. This stupid little bar that always kept her lights on, even when there was no electricity.

So why do I still love her? That's the easy part.
When the big bad bully came calling to flood and blow your house down, she knew it was her time to shine. She knew the importance of staying open for the people. After all weren't we all homeless, hungry and grief stricken! She knew the important role thrust upon her, handing out free food, water and most importantly, "We feel your pain conversation."

Even the other storm, the troopers with their guns, handcuffs and cameras in the tow, all gave up. And when she received national attention, didn't she make you smile, didn't she give you hope as you watched from you temporary home away from home. Didn't she make you proud if only for a moment, this defiant little girl who stood her ground!

Hell, someone had to stand up and spit into the eye of the storm. You weren't getting anything from our "blame game" politicians. Like the lyrics from our wonderful New Orleans song, "they're trying to wash us away."

Not today, Not tomorrow, Not My City!

I know this is stupid and I'm emotionally attached. She's like the pretty girl that breaks up with you and only time will heal.

When the final hours are ticking away and she's wondering what all the fuss is about, I'm gonna tell her there's another storm coming, I know what her response will be. "okay, I'll be ready!" Damn, dumb, stupid little bar.

If you'd like to say goodbye, please don't tell her why you're there. She's stubborn and wouldn't understand anyway.

Thanks Johnny
She loves you more

It was very touching, written from the heart, and the letter had everyone choked up. The bar was filled with copies, and one was taped, by the bartender on duty, to our French door window. The bar was filled with customers and employees in gray T-shirts sporting our ridiculously unattractive "Never Closed" sign with "Last Call" emblem superimposed over it. Some pictures and signs had already been removed from the walls, giving the bar a solemn feel.

A large canvas was hung in the back of the bar, covering one of the French doors, which made the bar dim and dark toward the back. However, everyone grabbed a marker and left their last farewell to the bar in graffiti on the canvas. Someone had made up signs for customers to hold that read "The End Is Near" and "Memory's Doors Never Close!"

As expected, people brought beach chairs and set up camp outside in anticipation for the closing ceremony and midnight march to MRB. Many regulars became frustrated with the scene. Lots of people in attendance were there because they just wanted to be part of the experience; they were strangers to those who frequented the bar. Locals and regulars found it difficult to get a drink inside at all and started going next door to Johnny White's Hole in the Wall for their cocktails, returning to their beach chairs to watch the scene from outside. No one really knew what to expect on this day, but for regulars, the "party" felt somewhat empty and anticlimactic. With not being able to get to the bar for a cocktail, the untraditional dark lighting with the canvas blocking the windows, empty walls with missing photos and artwork and strangers filling the walls, it was already not our bar.

When midnight came, one of the White family's bartenders came to put locks on the doors. Without much incident, we gathered the troops, and the second line band led us through the French Quarter to MRB. The band stayed for a while, playing in the street, and the party continued throughout the wee hours of the morning.

The next day, many people visited the locked shutters at J.W.'s and left flowers tucked in the locks or on the ground in front of the bar. And with that, the spirit of Johnny White's Sports Bar said goodbye and is forever gone.

While our sister bar, MRB, had been another favorite hangout for J.W.'s regulars, and they gave it a good go to let it replace the "locals' living room," for several reasons, it couldn't fill the sports bar's shoes. MRB attempted to stay open twenty-four hours to accommodate the sports bar's crowd, but the custom wasn't consistent, so after a short time, that fizzled out. However, when you wanted a taste of J.W.'s, MRB is where you might catch up with a few of the people who used to hold residence at J.W.'s.

Meanwhile, the White family renovated the corner bar, now called Johnny White's Corner Pub, into an attractive locale. It's much larger, as the bathroom behind the bar has been eliminated, leaving more room on

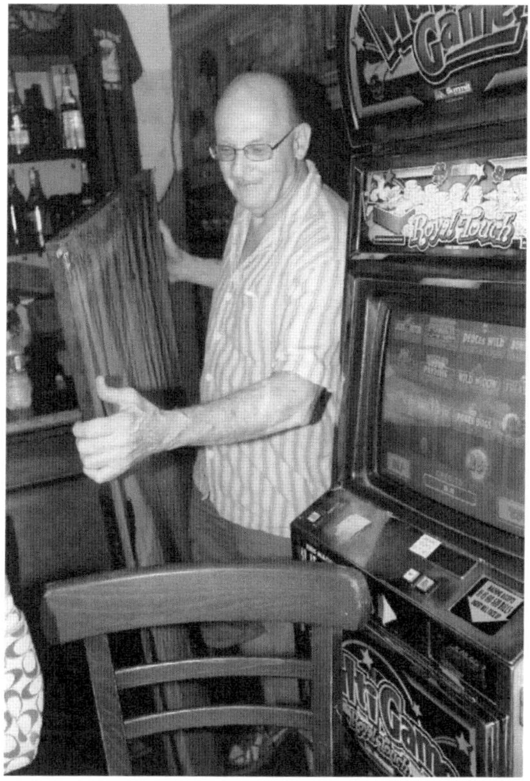

Right: Owner J.D. Landrum taking bar memorabilia out in anticipation of the bar's closure. *Moriah Blue.*

Below: Regulars during the last night at Johnny White's. *Byron Penn.*

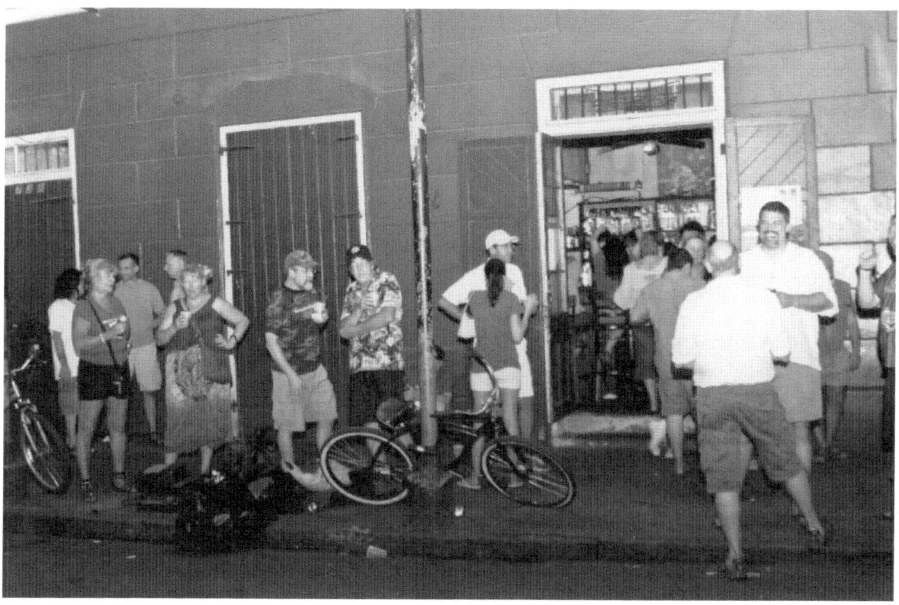

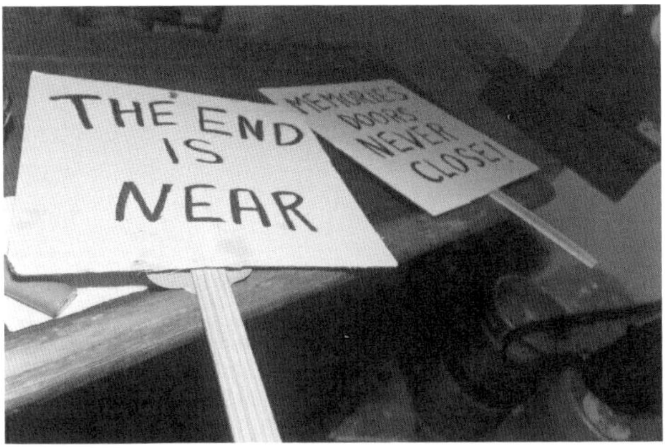

Left: Signs created for regulars to hold throughout the closing ceremony. *Moriah Blue.*

Below: Second line parade from Johnny White's through the Quarter to MRBs. *Moriah Blue.*

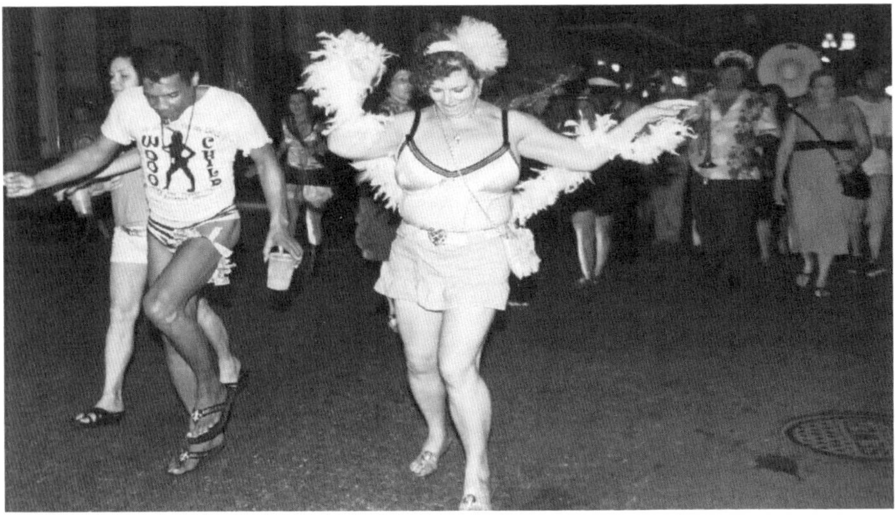

the floor for cocktail tables and chairs. The stairwell is now exposed, also giving the bar a much larger feel. Many of the old gang from J.W.'s stop in and have come to enjoy the bar. So, while the bar is beautiful and the view to Bourbon Street is the same, our old dingy bar will forever be in our hearts. I suppose the appropriate last words would be "Johnny White's Sports Bar is dead—long live Johnny White's Corner Pub!"

Afterword

Everyone who frequented Johnny White's has a story of their own, and if they have one, usually they have at least twenty. When I was new to the bar, I loved to sit around with the old-time regulars and listen to their stories. I was always envious that I had missed so much of what had transpired in the French Quarter before I even knew it existed. Ruthie the Duck Lady was just one character I enjoyed hearing about. As the years went by, and I encountered more and more characters and a plethora of memorable experiences unfolded before me, the stories piled up and I began to write a book I wanted to call *Drinking Mistakes*—a book about the experiences I had at Johnny White's while drinking all the mistakes I made in cocktails. However, after putting the book on the back burner for several years, as I picked it up again, I realized that the bar was more important than I ever realized. Rather than writing a book about my experiences, I should write a book about the bar's history, incorporating my experiences. That's how this book came to be.

That being said, I would like to share one of my favorite stories during my time at Johnny White's. It has no historical value and does not involve any local French Quarter characters, but it simply reminds me of what made the bar special and how much fun we had there. It will forever be a fond memory that still sometimes makes me laugh out loud when I think about it.

It was a pretty slow morning at J.W.'s. I had a couple of regulars in the bar, and we were probably chatting over a cocktail when one man entered

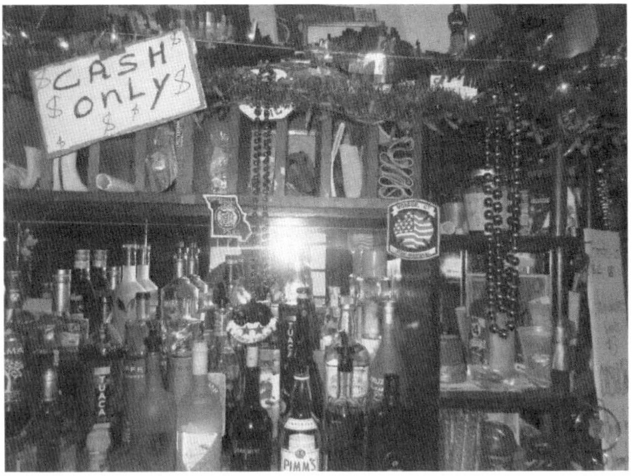

Area behind the bar filled with unusual objects. *Byron Penn.*

the bar accompanied by two women. One of the women turned out to be the man's wife and the other his sister. They all seemed to be in their late forties and were enjoying their morning on vacation in New Orleans. After getting a drink, the wife took a few dollars and started playing the poker machine, while the husband, sister and I shared a few stories. About a half an hour had gone by when we heard a ticket being printed from the poker machine. The wife came over and joined her husband, stood behind him and proudly handed me the poker ticket. "Do I redeem this here?" she asked. I took the ticket and looked at it. It was printed for the value of $3.50. Ordinarily, customers would bring us their tickets, usually for no less than $20, and usually for quite a bit more. It was not unusual that a customer would hit the machine for $500. But very rarely would anyone cash out a ticket for anything less than $20, unless they had made a mistake and hit the wrong button.

Well, I don't know what came over me, but I said, "Yes, you do!" I turned just behind me to the shelves on the corner edge behind the bar. It was where we had on display the famous "Never Closed Sign" and our "Cash Only" sign and three shelves that housed the most unusual cornucopia of bar paraphernalia: a wine bottle opener from the 1970s; several packs of plain white matchbooks, some of which Lulu, who was a bartender at the Johnny White's on Saint Peter, would decorate with little hand drawn pictures; dice we used during the graveyard shift; some old raffle tickets we used during Mardi Gras to give customers as receipts for bathroom access; an old golf ball; pens; a few strands of Mardi Gras beads; a couple of packs of open cigarettes that tourists left at the bar; the game "pigs"; paperclips; a couple of quarters; a Hawaiian lei from one of our theme parties; and a little stuffed Teddy bear sporting a Johnny White's Sports Bar T-shirt from Tammy's Teddy Bear store.

"You can pick anything on these shelves, except for the top shelf," I said. "For the Teddy bear, you would have to add six dollars." I wish I had a picture of the look on those three faces. I didn't break. We just stood there for a few seconds staring at each other. Then the wife hit her husband's shoulder and said, "Honey, you pick."

That's when I lost it. We all laughed, and she said, "I didn't think those were very good gifts".

Johnny White's Sports Bar, the tiny bar I thought I would never step foot into, became a spectacular chapter in my life that has greatly impacted who I have become.

Your Story Here:

About the Author

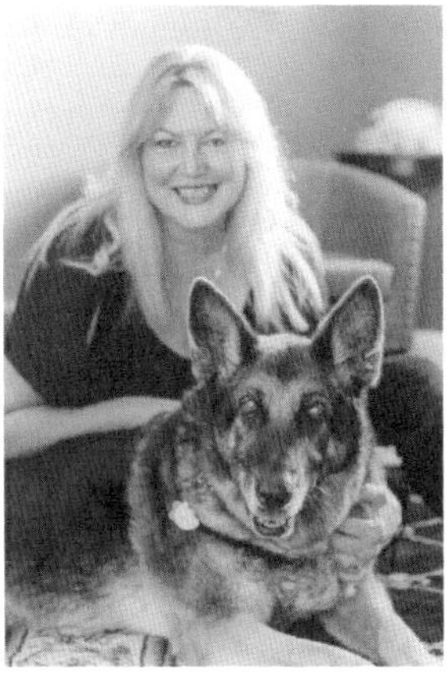

Marita is married to Steven Crandle of New Orleans, and together they run the Boutique du Vampyre and their vampire speakeasy, Potions.

Turbo Dog, named after a local Abita beer, worked at the sports bar with Marita daily. Turbo greeted people as they arrived, and he waited for his furry friends to come in with their owners throughout the day to socialize. Turbo inspired Marita to create the Johnny White's Canine Calendar, which was in production for ten years and raised money to help in Marita's dog rescue efforts to place over 650 dogs in loving homes, many of which were adopted by J.W. regulars.

Marita's book *New Orleans Vampires: History and Legend*, was also recently published through The History Press, and she is currently under contract with The History Press to write a historical book about the infamous Storyville madam Josie Arlington. Marita is also currently working on a historical fiction novel about the New Orleans vampire legend of The Carter Brothers.

Marita and her husband currently live both in the French Quarter and in Lake Front with their three rescued German Shepherds—Turbo Dog, Vilma and Atlas—and their rescued cockatiel, Voodoo.